London & The Home Counties Poets

Edited by Allison Jones

 Young**Writers**

First published in Great Britain in 2008 by:
Young Writers
Remus House
Coltsfoot Drive
Peterborough
PE2 9JX
Telephone: 01733 890066
Website: www.youngwriters.co.uk

SB ISBN 978-1 84431 457 7

Foreword

Young Writers was established in 1991 and has been passionately devoted to the promotion of reading and writing in children and young adults ever since. The quest continues today. Young Writers remains as committed to the nurturing of poetic and literary talent as ever.

This year's Young Writers competition has proven as vibrant and dynamic as ever and we are delighted to present a showcase of the best poetry from across the UK and in some cases overseas. Each poem has been selected from a wealth of *Little Laureates* entries before ultimately being published in this, our sixteenth primary school poetry series.

Once again, we have been supremely impressed by the overall quality of the entries we have received. The imagination, energy and creativity which has gone into each young writer's entry made choosing the poems a challenging and often difficult but ultimately hugely rewarding task - the general high standard of the work submitted ensured this opportunity to bring their poetry to a larger appreciative audience.

We sincerely hope you are pleased with this final collection and that you will enjoy *Little Laureates London & The Home Counties* for many years to come.

Contents

Fairley House School, London

Grange Park Junior School, Hayes

Hambrough Primary School, Southall

Longmead Primary School, West Drayton

Ben Steeples (10)   35
Ravinder Chopra (11)   35

Royston Primary School, London
Jamie Turnbull (7)   36
Jessica Maher (7)   36
Connor McKenna (7)   36
Tyrelle Thomas (7)   37
Tony Dowie (7)   37

St Elizabeth's Catholic Primary School, Richmond
Fergus O'Loan (9)   37
Honor Rudd (9)   38
Emily Wenman (9)   38
George Pearce (9)   38
Elena Garitta (9)   39
Alessandra Whelan Merediz (9)   39
Driéla Pereira Collins (9)   39
Lara Rogers (10)   40
Matthew Ilube (9)   40
Samuel MacKenzie (9)   40
Polly White (10)   41
Claudia Barron (10)   41
Kamil Suckocki (9)   41
Lauren Flynn (10)   42
Lauren Donaldson (9)   42
Raquel Traseira Pedraz (9)   43
Thalia Kent-Egan (9)   43
Conor O'Hara (9)   44
Millie Brogden (9)   44
Daniel O'Sullivan (9)   44
Katie Duffy (10)   45
Antonia Ruddle (9)   45
Hamish Macleod (9)   45
Archie Adams (9)   46
Esme Rogers (8)   46
Sebastien Byrnes Soler (9)   46
Henry Sempers-Spangenberg (8)   46
Jasmine Rienecker (8)   47
Sean Mackenzie (8)   47
Thomas Pongrácz (8)   47

Hannah Griggs & Victoria Partridge (10)   63
Lydia Johnston (9) & Beatrice Taylor (10)   64
Luke Hoesli (9)   64
Francesca Lovell (9) & Grace Brixton (10)   65

Sparrow Farm Community Junior School, Stoneleigh
Sophie Purdy (10)   65
Hollie Drewett (10)   66
Jordan Heavens (10)   66
Anna Seddon (10)   67
Piers Reucroft (10)   67
Brandon Robins (10)   68
Owen Chan (10)   68
Nicki Erodotou (10)   69
Alfie Stockwell (11)   69
Robert Mutch (10)   70
Trinidad Challenger (10)   70
Thanzil Uddin (10)   70
Clara Gibson (10)   71
Sam Jenkins (10)   71
Hollie Egremont (11)   71
Alainna Chambers (10)   72
Laxsica Ranjan (11)   72
Charlotte Gosling (10)   73
Hannah Jarvis (10)   73
Kayoon Kim (10)   73
Hannah Stone (10)   74
Hannah Rowe (10)   74
Loran Chambers (10)   75
Sue-ling Chan-Wyles (10)   75
Tara Evlambiou (11)   76
Dominic Pencherz (10)   76
Saffron Armstrong (10)   77
Edgar Gomes (11)   77
Hayley Burden (10)   78
Luke Boulton (10)   78
Billy Collier (10)   79
Freddie Finnett (10)   79
Joshua Bull (11)   80
Chloe Hudson (10)   81
Oscar Stewart (10)   82

Callum McCarthy (11)	82
Curtis Gore (11)	82
Elena Hoskins (10)	83
Ethan Hogan (10)	83
Phoebe Frewin (10)	84
Harrison Pike (11)	84
Ryan Humphryes (10)	85
Simon Hickman (10)	85
William Cunningham (10)	86
Michelle Sharpe (10)	86
Jed Thomas (11)	87
Shehnaz Aziz (10)	87
Precious Opara (10)	88
Joseph Phillips (10)	88
Chloe Kirby (11)	89
Georgina Baxter (10)	89
Adam Levett & Zavien Smith (10)	90
Nayyara Malik (10)	90
Myles Mitchell (10)	91

The Harrodian School, Barnes

Lizzie Melville (9)	91
Robert McBride (9)	91
Charlie Clark (9)	92
Sebastian Williams (10)	93
Max Cranmer (10)	94
Anna Carruthers (9)	94
James Odgers (9)	95
Jacob Patmore (9)	95
Imagen Powell (8)	96
Charlotte Birtles (9)	96
Charlie Nason (10)	97
Zoë Spurgeon (9)	97
Sasha Vergopoulos (10)	98
Olivia van Meeteren (9)	98
Aimee Van der Merwe (10)	99
Luke Finckenstein (10)	99
Edward Cadbury (10)	100
Connie O'Neill (10)	100
Isabella Gasparro (10)	101
Sophia Brown (10)	101

The Poems

Artist's Palette

An artist's palette is like a rainbow
Spreading out under the dome of the sky.
The blue is like a deep, deep sea
Where the mermaids sing.
The green is like a forest
Full of chirping birds.
The yellow is like the fiery, blazing sun
Burning in the sky.
The red is like sweet-smelling roses
Blooming in a beautiful garden.
The white is like the snow falling
Thick and fast on a cold winter's day.
The black is like the night sky
Sparkling with stars that shimmer like diamonds.
An artist's palette is like a rainbow
Spreading out to its magical pot of gold.

Charlotte Benham (9)
Bengeo Primary School, Hertford

Ellie And The Wellie

There was a young girl called Ellie,
Who jumped into a pool on her belly.
One day in the pool
She was doing front crawl
And someone threw her a wellie!

Ella Mitham (9)
Bengeo Primary School, Hertford

Autumn Leaves

In the woods I can see
Golden leaves, a canopy above,
Red and yellow,
Brown and green
Are the colours I can see.

Dancing leaves, a knotted tree,
All these things around me,
Russet, crimson, amber and gold,
Purple, black, they all unfold.

On the floor and up above,
Flying away like a dove,
All the colours,
Red, yellow and green,
Are some of the colours I have seen.

Matthew Pizzey (9)
Bengeo Primary School, Hertford

The Snowflake

I once saw a snowflake called Snow,
Who fell from the sky like a crow.
When she hit the ground,
A bird turned around
And did a big poo on my toe!

Charlotte Lee (10)
Bengeo Primary School, Hertford

Mary The Fairy

There was a young girl called Mary,
Who magically turned into a fairy.
She granted a wish
Which turned into a fish,
But it was very scary!

Sam Rix (9)
Bengeo Primary School, Hertford

Autumn Woods

The wood is a mysterious place,
Bees buzz around with surprising grace.
Further on, I see golden leaves
Falling off gnarled old oak trees.
Deeper and deeper I go into the wood,
I look up into the canopy
And I see leaves like a golden hood.
I hear birds singing,
Twigs snapping,
Dogs barking,
Leaves rustling.
Autumn is here!

Ewan Thomas-Colquhoun (9)
Bengeo Primary School, Hertford

Socks

Socks, so warm and comfy,
They keep me from the horrible feel
Of the carpet on my bare feet
And from blisters from my shoes.
Oh no . . . oh no . . . *ouch!*

They come in lots of colours,
Different sizes and shapes,
Exciting patterns and designs,
So they will suit you . . .
And you . . . and you . . . great!

Sophie Rawlinson (9)
Bengeo Primary School, Hertford

My Dog Mylo

Mylo is my dog,
He often attacks trees.
He snorts like a pig
In the cool breeze.

Mylo is orange,
He eats lots of meat.
He sleeps in the kitchen
And loves to have a treat.

Mylo goes on walks
And weighs almost three stone.
When he jumps on the sofa,
Mum always starts to moan.

Mylo chews my toys
And nibbles Stevie's ears.
When we went on holiday,
We found out he doesn't like piers!

Millie Salmons (10)
Bengeo Primary School, Hertford

Dan The Man!

There once was a man named Dan,
Who wanted to live with his nan.
He went to her house,
Got shot by a mouse
And drove away in his van.

Sarah Cassidy (10)
Bengeo Primary School, Hertford

Autumn Days

When I went into the woods,
The magic had just started.
Little birds in the treetops,
Swooped and then they darted.
Tiny dewdrops sparkling in the sun,
Then I knew the magic had begun!

Leaves as delicate as thin paper,
Yellow, crimson, russet and green.
Then I saw the toadstool queen.
Toadstools like bubbles on a tree stump,
Leaves piled up in a hump.

Sunlight coming through in chinks,
Raindrops falling like dripping sinks,
A light mist covered the sun,
The magic has finished just as it had begun.

Madeleine Twyning (9)
Bengeo Primary School, Hertford

The Cat Called Fred

There once was a cat called Fred,
Who had his very own bed.
He had a saucer of milk,
Liked dressing in silk,
And once climbed up on my head!

Sophie Shaw (9)
Bengeo Primary School, Hertford

Crazy Animals

An elephant lived in the park,
Because he'd been scared by the shark.
He ran back to the zoo
And he shouted, 'Boohoo,'
Then haunted them all for a lark!

Jessica Ensum (9)
Bengeo Primary School, Hertford

My Autumn Garden

Shining blue sky,
Fluffy white clouds,
Green, green leaves,
Yellow sunlight,
Golden trees,
What a sight!
Beautiful autumn,
A real delight!

Jordan Ellis (9)
Bengeo Primary School, Hertford

My Magic Box

This is my magic box,
You'll never know what's in store.
Ice cream, cakes and sweeties,
There's all that and more.
It's always fun in my magic box,
There's loads of things to do,
Parks, funfairs and a circus
And they're all things for . . . *you!*

Grace Shallis (9)
Christopher Rawlins CE(A) Primary School, Banbury

Magic Box

Stamford Bridge is the place I go,
To see the Blues put on a show.

If I sing and cheer, and shout out loud,
The boys in blue will do me proud.

Lampard, Drogba, Sheva and Cole,
They're the ones that will score us a goal.

Arsenal 0, Chelsea 4,
That was my dream, and the final score.

That is what's in my magic box,
And I'll always love it lots!

Lewis Bullard (10)
Christopher Rawlins CE(A) Primary School, Banbury

The Skeletons

In the dark of the night while you sleep,
A strange, spooky dance you must see.
Silhouettes of white scare you alive,
Bones and skulls come alive.
The skeletons prance and dance around,
No sound they make,
Putting you in a trance.
As morning breaks, to bed they slither,
Back to their coffins, all cold with shivers.

George Ding (9)
Christopher Rawlins CE(A) Primary School, Banbury

Magic Box

My magic box is fantastic,
The things you find are bombastic.
When I open my box my thoughts go flying around,
I can see all the pictures and hear all the sound.

I am going to talk about a club called Arsenal,
There is no one better on the ball.
Rosicky has a rocket shot,
The goalkeeper has a shock.

Now my box shows me scoring a try,
In a rugby match I dive and fly.
All the tries are scored by me,
I get the conversion with a kicking tee.

That's the end of my magic box,
You can listen in your socks.
Why don't you join me
And don't go away and flee!

Joshua Gibbins (9)
Christopher Rawlins CE(A) Primary School, Banbury

My Magic Box

In my magic box there is a secret beyond compare,
It would make your spine shiver
And make you want to scream,
So listen if you dare,
But be warned, this secret is yet to be told,
And beware, this secret will make
The winds howl and doors shut,
And sometimes you can hear Lady Jane scream in pain, but why?
So open it if you dare.
That is what is in my magic box.

Hope Barton (9)
Christopher Rawlins CE(A) Primary School, Banbury

Magic Box

In my magic box I found a puppy,
I think that I am very lucky.
He has big brown eyes and floppy ears,
I'm so glad that Puppy is here.

I've been wishing and waiting and asking out loud.
With my brand new puppy, I'm so very proud.
I'll take him for walks and we'll play in the rain,
He will fetch sticks again and again.

My puppy is cute and very kind
And sometimes he is hard to find.
My puppy is very small,
Unlike some other dogs which are really tall.

My puppy has a brown coat
And a little white patch on his throat.
With his wagging tail and very cute paws,
I hope he doesn't scratch the doors.

Zoe Edwards (9)
Christopher Rawlins CE(A) Primary School, Banbury

My Magic Box

In my magic box there are
Powerful horses that run across the evergreen meadows.
In my magic box there are
Millions of birds that fly high across the endless blue sky.
In my magic box there are
Silver-coated elephants that jump through the mysterious dark jungle.
In my magic box there are
Multicoloured fish that leap out of the shining blue sea.
In my magic box there are
Smooth blue and grey dolphins that take you
On adventurous sea rides.
My magic box is the most wonderful box
On the planet, and it's all mine!

Liza Arts (9)
Christopher Rawlins CE(A) Primary School, Banbury

My Magic Box

In my magic box are my magic pets,
Named Emma, Cocoa and Pansy.
One is a dog, the other two hamsters,
But all of them equally great.
When I open the box they are miniature,
When I make them jump out they become full-size.
It gave me a shock at first, but now it just gives me a surprise!

My magic dog Emma is the best dog ever,
But she's even better because . . .
She runs so fast, she could time-travel to the past
And take off in the air like no dog's done before!
That's why I chose her to do my chores!

My hamsters, on the other hand, are peaceful and quiet,
They don't run around making a riot.
Instead they just sit, or play in their wheels,
Or play in their balls, or eat apple peels.
Don't interrupt them, they're trying to sleep,
They're trying to sleep in their beds in a heap.

Amelia Morgan (9)
Christopher Rawlins CE(A) Primary School, Banbury

I Wonder What's In My Magic Box?

Conkers falling down from the trees,
Close the windows, days are getting colder,
Trees are getting older,
Coats coming off the pegs,
Hallowe'en coming, Bonfire Night too,
Harvest just gone,
Floating, flying leaves as colourful and bright as
Fireworks and shooting stars.
Have you guessed what is in my magic box?
Autumn, of course!

Olivia O'Donoghue (10)
Christopher Rawlins CE(A) Primary School, Banbury

My Magic Box

I carry my tack,
A carrot,
A whip,
But deep inside my pocket,
There's something I've hid.

My horse, Stargazer,
Is waiting,
Anticipating,
I'll say the magic turning spell
So he can talk to me.

In his true form
As a unicorn
He can fly,
No ordinary horse,
My magical unicorn.

Changed by the words
Written in the magic box,
Stargazer,
My horse,
My secret unicorn.

Jodie Goffe (10)
Christopher Rawlins CE(A) Primary School, Banbury

What Is In My Magic Box? - Cinquain

Ice cream,
Fun in the sun,
Golden sands and blue seas,
Barbecues and holidays,
Summer.

Luca De-Meis (9)
Christopher Rawlins CE(A) Primary School, Banbury

My Magic Box

I have a special magic box
That sits upon my shelf.
It's red and gold, green and black,
And opens by itself!

Inside you'll find my special friend,
Ginger is his name,
He's a cute and fluffy hamster
And he has a claim to fame!

He's really great at climbing,
In fact he is the best.
He holds the hamster world record
For climbing Mount Everest!

But be careful not to scare him
Or he'll bite you with his teeth.
For although he might be famous,
He's a monster underneath!

George Heath (9)
Christopher Rawlins CE(A) Primary School, Banbury

My Magic Box

Aston Villa are the best,
To beat them is a test.
We sometimes win, we sometimes lose,
The opposing crowd give us boos.
Our players are great and our manager's fab,
If we win the Premiership, I will be glad.
Aston Villa are the best,
To beat them is a test.
One day when we win this trophy,
The other teams will bow down on one knee.
My magic box is a treasure to me,
My magic box always will be.

Brandon Haden (9)
Christopher Rawlins CE(A) Primary School, Banbury

Magic Box

I have a magic box,
My best friend gave it to me.
When I opened it up,
I saw a little puppy.

In my magic box
There can be anything, you see.
All I have to do is think
And the only one who could do that is me.

I hold my box in my hands
And wish for a surprise.
Then I see a flash of light
Before my very eyes.

Holly Smith (9)
Christopher Rawlins CE(A) Primary School, Banbury

Magic Box

Cricket's my game,
Many wickets are my aim.
When I bat I score no more than four,
But when I try, I get so many more!

When I'm older I want to keep,
England is what I seek.
When I keep, I stop byes,
But if I don't my teammates sigh.

When we win I'm really glad,
When we lose I'm really sad.
Cricket is really special to me
And a cricketer is all I want to be!

Jack Lambden (9)
Christopher Rawlins CE(A) Primary School, Banbury

My Magic Box

What is inside my magic box?
A small, furry kitten
Tucked up with its mum,
All nice and warm,
Just like the heat of the sun.
Eyes closed up tight
As it is so young.
Its fur is soft and many colours,
It cannot do anything wrong.
Oh how I love my little kitten,
I shall name her Emily.
Night, night, my little kitten,
I am also feeling very sleepy.
Time to close my box.

Emily Source (9)
Christopher Rawlins CE(A) Primary School, Banbury

My Rabbits

I've got some rabbits,
I love them very much,
They live in the garden
In a two-storey hutch.

They're always on the go,
They like to run fast,
Round and round the garden,
Stopping only to eat fresh grass.

Their ears are long,
They point to the sky,
They'd better behave
Or they will end up in a pie!

Gemma Eley (9)
Christopher Rawlins CE(A) Primary School, Banbury

Step Into My Paradise

Pretty pink flowers were glamorous fluttering birds,
Flowers were the prettiest colours you've ever seen.
The archway is as eye-catching as Tower Bridge,
With beautiful lights flashing out in beams.

A tranquil, peaceful fragrance bursting out of a new bud,
As peaceful as my house at night.
There isn't a place where you'll find mud,
Yes! It's out of sight.

My garden is great,
It is better than the rest,
I love it so much.

Children climb up my body
And crawl on my arms.
Little drops of flakes fall from my head
And gently descend to the ground.

Green grass grows gently
Beside the flower beds.
Caring crows croak away;
Whilst I rest my peaceful head.

Tender loving care
Is what my garden has here,
As I brush my hair.

Leslie Bonlong (11)
Elfrida Primary School, Bellingham

My Paradise

Roses red as rubies,
Swaying in the flower bed.
Next to it a water fountain
With a statue of a fish that's red.

Green grass growing gracefully,
Butterflies flying high in the sky,
Little bunnies bouncing everywhere,
A hedge as circular as a pie.

The garden is so tranquil,
The daffodil is a gleaming sun,
The fragrance is so sweet,
You get the taste of an iced bun.

I love my garden,
It is extremely peaceful,
It is beautiful.

The pond is as blue as the deep blue sea,
The fish inside it are swimming
And they look up at me.
I find them so amazing.

Lots of bright colours
In this garden surrounding me.
I find it such fun
With the water fountain as blue as the sea.

Rebecca Adnett (11)
Elfrida Primary School, Bellingham

My Garden

A fountain as outstanding
As a colourful rainforest,
Roses as red as poppies
Surrounding the aquatic fountain.

The garden is humungous and beautiful,
It feels like you're in paradise.
You can hear birds singing
As you sit there in the peaceful garden.

My garden is lovely.
In the flower bed the flowers sway.
As the sun glimmers on the flower bed,
The fragrance of the garden is so strong you can taste it.

As everyone's fast asleep, the moon rises,
The foxes come out to play.
As the year passes round, the leaves
Drop off the tree, as light as feathers.

Chantelle Bromwell (10)
Elfrida Primary School, Bellingham

My Garden

The grandfather clock is tall like a tower,
All it does is sit quietly.
The flowers are colourful like butterflies.

The fountain is crystal-white like a polar bear,
The lawn is tidy like the Queen's house,
The bushes are as prickly as a cactus.

The leaves on the trees are as light as a feather,
They come in all different colours.
The daffodils are as yellow as the sun.

Kelsey Schafer-Nolan (10)
Elfrida Primary School, Bellingham

An Object From Tom's Midnight Garden

What a nice day it is; my hands sparkle like a mirror.
I feel a little breeze.
Huh, Tom? What are you doing?
Coming to fill me up, hey?
Ah, perfect. Ow, a bit hot don't you think?
Hello? Put some cold in me now!
Hello? A bit too hot.
That's better.
Huh, what? Stop getting unchanged.
Hey, Toilet, close your mouth.
Ew, you're in the nude.
I feel sick. Hey, what are you doing?
Leave Soap alone. Soap, are you OK? I feel sorry for you.
You have to go up and down everywhere.
Hey, it stinks! I'm not a Jacuzzi, get out of me, now!
Did I scare him away?
Good.
Hey, what are you doing? You're taking the warmth out of me.
I wish I was in bath heaven.
I'm as dirty as a pig having a mud bath.

Rebecca Taylor (10)
Elfrida Primary School, Bellingham

Peter's Measles

Come on, Peter, scratch me, be a man.
Why not scratch me? Don't be a chicken.
If you don't scratch, I'll turn as red as a baboon's bum!
Don't make me angry, you won't like me when I'm angry.
Don't be a mummy's boy.
Don't make me get my dad, he's double my size.
I look like a river of volcanoes, don't you want me gone?
Peter, scratch me, just this once,
Scratch me if you want me gone.

Joseph Johnson (10)
Elfrida Primary School, Bellingham

Girl's Book

You, over there, yeah you,
You're new to the family;
I haven't seen anybody for years.
That's it, come here, yeah.
Pick me up, yes, you picked me.
Stop playing with my eyelashes,
They are as thin as pancakes, you know.
I'm as smooth as silk.
Don't you dare say those nasty words about me!
I'm a river of words inside,
Don't judge me by my face.
Hey, don't throw me violently on the floor!
Ow, my back, I'm in so much pain.
I'm so sad.
My life is horrible, probably going to be
Left alone for about another twenty years now.

Jade Butler (10)
Elfrida Primary School, Bellingham

An Object From Tom's Midnight Garden

'Atchoo!' I wish someone would get the dust off me.
Who do you think you are?
I have delicate skin, so don't throw me on the floor.
Hey, Tom, look here, I'm with my friends;
Can you read me?
Why are you not reading me?
I'm going to cry now.
What are you doing lying on your bed?
I'm as cold as an ice cube.
Come and put your hands around me.
I'm as colourful as a rainbow,
I'm as hard as wood,
My skin is as thin as wafers.

Tiffany Farley (10)
Elfrida Primary School, Bellingham

The Bed

Ah, what a beautiful morning.
Hey, I'm empty!
Tom, where are you?

I'm so lonely,
I feel as neglected as a lost puppy.
Come on, lay on me, I'm so cold.

Hey, Peter, get off me!
I don't want your measles!
Oh I'm starting to feel itchy!

Come on, you know you want to lie on me,
I'm a rectangle of warmth!
Come on, it will be your best sleep in ages!
Give in to your temptation!

Oh, and I'm sick and tired of your mum crying into me,
I'm so wet; I look like I've had an accident!
You know, she's not the only one who misses you!

Leyla Sakiroglu (11)
Elfrida Primary School, Bellingham

The Stairs

What a gorgeous morning.
Just because you're jealous,
Doesn't mean you can trample on me!
Oi! Don't tread on me, you dirty thing!

Ah, I could relax all day long.
It's a beautiful afternoon.
Oh no! Not you again,
Don't you come near me.

It's night now, I can sleep.
My soft blanket will keep me warm.
I am a baby's blanket.
I could sleep all day but instead I sleep at night.

Alex Hotca (10)
Elfrida Primary School, Bellingham

Peter's Measles

Hey you, Peter, scratch me.
You know you want to.
I'll turn red like a baboon's buttocks!
If you put cream on,
I'll go to your personal weak spot.

Come on, scratch me, or I'll spread out more babies.
Come on, are you a little mummy's boy?
Peter, please, I'll go red as chilli peppers,
You'll have to scratch me then.

I'm as bumpy as a camel's hump.
Come on, I'm waiting for my massage.
I'm a mouse trapped in a cage.

Tony To (10)
Elfrida Primary School, Bellingham

Tom's Slipper

I wake up and have a yawn like a tired baby.
A little break to just relax
Next to my brother,
Praying he doesn't pick me.

Oi, stop coming closer,
Get your big feet out of me!
Stop treading on me, I'm not grass.

I do have feelings you know!
Don't smash me down like a ball.
I don't believe you still love me, do you?
Back to sleep again,
Dreading tomorrow in case it happens again.

Luke Cullen (11)
Elfrida Primary School, Bellingham

The Door To The Garden

I'm tall and very firm,
As brown as chocolate,
As I sit here patiently
Waiting for a visitor.

I'm as hard as a turtle's shell,
But still I cannot move.
Sadly, I'm never noticed,
But only walked past.

I'm rusty, never washed,
But sometimes painted.
I am a guard
Protecting the house.

I could be ninety years old,
However I still never die.
I live forever,
Although I will soon be knocked down.

My cousin stops me from moving
By locking me up.
When I have been scratched,
I am left there to rot.

Tyrell Robinson (10)
Elfrida Primary School, Bellingham

Aunt Gwen's Food

I'm hot just like the sun,
Come eat me if you dare, wimp.
Put me in your mouth and taste the flavour,
You are my best friend.

I'm as delightful as a five-star hotel.
Come on, you know you want me.
She's going to throw me away.

I thought you were my friend,
Why are you doing this to me?
I'm the tastiest thing you've ever tasted,
Leave me and I'll grow hair.

Come on, come on, give me your best shot.
Help, help, she's throwing me away, help!
Come on, you don't want to do this.
I thought you were my friend!

Eat me while I'm hot,
Please don't leave me!
I'll do anything. Help, help!
You know I'm a fountain of taste and smell.

Jade Lay (10)
Elfrida Primary School, Bellingham

Tom's Real Bed

Tom, Tom, where are you?
Come on, this isn't funny.
Stop scaring me. Where are you going?
Don't leave me.

I'm a lonely, lost child;
I am a table of silk - you know you love me.
You're the only one I like to hold.

Why won't anyone massage me?
I'm the only river of dreams in town.
I feel like a washing line with no clothes on it.

You know what? When you come back,
Don't expect to lay on me.
Go on, go away, but watch when you come back,
I'll show you what I'm made of.

What does the other bed you're laying on smell like?
A hundred red roses?
Well I'm as bouncy as a trampoline, but not for you!
I'm going to live a happy life - without you!

Chloe Power (10)
Elfrida Primary School, Bellingham

The Girl Books

It's pitch-black in this cupboard,
It's been years since I've been read.
I wonder why Aunt Gwen does not read me?

Who's coming? Oh, I hope it's Aunt Gwen.
Light! I can see again!
That's not Aunt Gwen, oh well.
Pick me, don't pick Cinderella;
She's so mind-numbingly boring,
I am a pretty pink pearl in the bottom of the sea.

Yes, I'm picked.
How dare you look at me like that?
Ow, that hurt!
My pages are as thin as a strand of hair, you know?

You messed up my hair,
My story is like a trapped fairy tale now.
Who do you think you are?
You think you can just waltz yourself in here.
Even if you don't want to read me, just clean me.

I feel like a baby with no mum.
I . . . I hate you! Get out of here!

Rhonda Cowell (10)
Elfrida Primary School, Bellingham

An Object From Tom's Midnight Garden

Hey, Tom, look down here,
I'm so covered in dust that you can't see
My beautiful sky-blue colour.
Cheer up and say hello,
It's boring sitting under the bed.
I'm as soft as a baby's bottom.
Come on, let's go for a walk,
I would like to go for a walk in the garden.
It's dark as a cave under here,
Can you give me some attention, please?
At last, he is awake now.
Oh no! His feet are cold.
I hope he washed his feet.
Yuck! They smell like rotten cheese.

Michelle Pons (11)
Elfrida Primary School, Bellingham

Peter's Measles

I am a river of camel humps and often get teased.
I always get scratched and hurt.
Ouch, that hurt! Get your hand away from me.
Excuse me, you're pulling my skin off.
Please don't hurt me, I'm contagious for a reason.
I'm gonna get angry and tell Tom to never come home,
You'll stop scratching me then.
Just tell me something,
Why do you always scratch me and no one else?
Don't you like me giving you some colour?
I feel picked on these days.
I bring no harm,
I'm only a red, miniature hill.

Jessica Miller (10)
Elfrida Primary School, Bellingham

Super Space Journey

On my magic carpet, hurtling through the air,
I saw a huge, hot, beaming sun.
I was so excited, I almost fell off my magic carpet.
Then I suddenly felt something coming towards me.
What was it?
I was really scared.
Then I saw it, it was a fiery rocket.
All of a sudden, I couldn't see anything,
It was pitch-black.
There was no sound.
A dark moon appeared,
I was fearful.
Eventually I landed.
I heard gigantic noises.
I was touching something slimy,
There was a horrible smell,
I was feeling very worried.
I was also really happy,
I was finally on the sun.

Chloe Tyler (8)
Elfrida Primary School, Bellingham

The Golden Sun

Flying on a magic carpet,
I feel excited.
I feel scared going over the moon.
I feel happy.
I feel over the moon!
Flying high over the golden sun
It brings tears of joy to my eyes.

Chloe Slynes (9)
Elfrida Primary School, Bellingham

The Fire Planet

On my shooting star, hurtling around the beaming sun,
I felt over the moon!
But suddenly I approached a black hole.
I shivered like I was at the North Pole.
I felt all wobbly like jelly,
But I saw the sparkly moon!

Sedanur Gurbuz (8)
Elfrida Primary School, Bellingham

Ruby

The shimmering
Ruby, red,
The blossoming,
Blood-sodden crystal
Sparkles
In my dirty bare hand.

Lindsay Hogg-Thomason (10)
Fairley House School, London

The Leaky Kennel

Ben is a dog,
He lives in a kennel,
He does not like it,
It leaks.
He uses leaves,
It does not work.
He uses sticks,
But that does not work,
The leak is too strong.
What can he do?

Max Rubens (9)
Fairley House School, London

The Journey

I can see mayhem.
The waves are getting bigger and bigger.
Ropes hang loose.
Dark clouds surround us, as far as the eye can see.
It is dark.
I can only hear the waves and wind.
The captain is shouting but I cannot hear him.
I feel damp and cold. My head is pounding.

I touch the mast,
It is cold and damp. It is moving.
I taste the salty sea,
I smell the salt.

Harry Penrice (11)
Fairley House School, London

Cat In The Window

What do I hear?

I can hear the stars twinkling brightly,
While a wolf is howling angrily,
The clock ticking silently and slowly.
I can hear a cat purring softly,
The rain dripping gently on the slippery road
As cars whizz by happily.

I can her the milkman whistling quietly, like a bird,
An old man is snoring loudly.
Children walking joyfully and smartly,
As a dog grumbles piercingly and bravely.

I can hear . . .

Jinoshan Anton (10)
Grange Park Junior School, Hayes

Cat In The Window

What do I hear?

A mouse squeaking in fear,
An angry voice coming from above the living room,
The clock ticking over and over again,
Tick-tock, tick-tock.

I hear . . .

Creepy, ghostly, terrifying noises,
A dog barking menacingly,
My owner's bad snoring upstairs,
A dreadful singing.

I hear . . .

Siobhan MacKenzie (9)
Grange Park Junior School, Hayes

Vampire

Vampire,
Blood-curdling, menacing, horrific,
Creeping mysteriously down the hallway.
Fright renders me speechless.
Bloodthirsty nightmare.

Nidah Sandhu (10)
Grange Park Junior School, Hayes

Cat In The Window

What do I hear?

A car zooming down the silent road,
Trees swaying in the light, soft breeze,
Raindrops tipping down the glass pane.

I hear . . .

Children running down the street,
A baby crying in the middle of the night,
The rain thundering heavily.

I hear . . .

Sukhmit Kaur Bharj (9)
Grange Park Junior School, Hayes

Cat In The Window

What do I hear?

My owner snoring in the dark night,
The grandfather clock striking midnight.

I hear . . .

Cars darting on the slippery road,
Next-door's dog fiercely barking at the cars roaring past.

I hear . . .

Alfie Martin (10)
Grange Park Junior School, Hayes

Cat In The Window

What do I hear?

Thunder roaring like a giant,
A baby crying.

I hear . . .
Joyful raindrops dancing on the ground.
As the rain falls, cars start sliding
And a dog splashes at midnight.

I hear . . .

Thushani Muruganantharajah (9)
Grange Park Junior School, Hayes

Friendship

When I read these words today,
They made me think of you
And the memories we share
That will last a long time.

I know that our friendship
Our whole lives through will last,
And we'll be loved just as much
When today becomes the past.

Thenujah Kuganeswaran (9)
Grange Park Junior School, Hayes

Sound Of Silence

Can you hear me remembering
The lovely white sand in Turkey?
Can you hear me remembering
The fast hip hop song?
Can you hear me remembering
The enjoyable game that we played at playtime?
Can you hear me remembering
When my brother was finally brought into this world/
Can you hear me imagining,
Hoping for my dreams to come true?
Can you her me imagining
That beautiful sandy beach on the edge of Greece?
Can you hear me imagining
Being a tiny, glittery fairy fluttering my shiny wings in the moonlight?
Can you hear me imagining
What I would look like if I was a princess?
Can you hear me thinking
Of the dreamland that has a throne that awaits me?
Can you hear me thinking
What it would be like to wear that breathtaking dress?
Can you hear me thinking
What it would be like if I travelled into space?
Can you hear me thinking
What it would be like to see kangaroos and koalas in Australia?
Can you hear me listening
To the leaves rustling in the wind?
Can you hear me listening
To the waves rushing to the shore?
Can you hear me listening
To the branches of trees swaying in the warm breeze?
Can you hear me listening
To the mobile vibrating on the glass table?

Alisha Janjua (10)
Hambrough Primary School, Southall

Seasons

The year starts with spring.
Flowers start to grow,
Blossom on the trees,
Sometimes it snows.

Then comes summer,
Our holidays start soon,
Lots of sunshine, lots of sand,
I love June.

Next comes autumn,
Leaves begin to fall,
Getting dark early,
Early to bed for school.

Now we're into winter,
The days are really cold,
Our coats and hats are needed
Or you'll look very wrinkly and old.

Leah Steeples (10)
Longmead Primary School, West Drayton

Louise

L ovely Louise,
O val face,
U nusual young lady,
I   nteresting but
S mart and sweet,
E nergetic.

Louise Whitby (8)
Longmead Primary School, West Drayton

Snake

Snake stayed camouflaged in the grass
Until some prey came slowly past.
Snake thought it was really funny
When he only caught a chocolate bunny!

Snake was searching in the grass
Until some prey caught his eye at last.
Snake didn't think it was really funny
When he was trying to fit a dinosaur in his tummy!

Fahim Ahmed (9)
Longmead Primary School, West Drayton

Bye Rabbit!

Rabbit, Rabbit, oh how can you see?
Rabbit, Rabbit who could I be?
Rabbit, Rabbit, oh why can't you see?
Rabbit, Rabbit, will you come with me?

Rabbit, Rabbit, why did you leave me?
Rabbit, Rabbit, why wouldn't you stay?
Rabbit, Rabbit I know why you died.
Rabbit, Rabbit, you had a good life.

Ben Steeples (10)
Longmead Primary School, West Drayton

I Love You

If you are in my life,
I want to take you as my wife.
Without you in my destiny,
My whole life will go plainly.
So if you think this poem's fine,
I want you to be mine.

Ravinder Chopra (11)
Longmead Primary School, West Drayton

Foods

Apples are as red as a fire engine,
Pears are as green as the grass,
Jelly is like jam,
Orange is like the sunset,
Ham is as pink as a pig,
Lemons are as yellow as the sun,
Ice cream is as cold as winter,
Grapes are as purple as plums.

Jamie Turnbull (7)
Royston Primary School, London

My Best Food

Bananas are as soft as cushions,
Cherries are like red balls,
Crisps are as crunchy as cookies,
Chips are like yellow sticks,
Ice is like a solid cube.

Jessica Maher (7)
Royston Primary School, London

Food

Apples are as green as the grass,
Jelly is as sweet as jam,
Carrots are pointy like cats' whiskers,
Pears are like a pig's tail,
Blueberries are as blue as the sky.

Connor McKenna (7)
Royston Primary School, London

Sweet Food

Apples are as juicy as strawberries,
Pancakes are as nice as pears,
Ice creams are as cold as snowflakes,
Carrots are as delicious as bananas,
Blueberries are as sweet as oranges,
Cakes are as nice as chicken!

Tyrelle Thomas (7)
Royston Primary School, London

Food Poem

Yoghurt is as nice as a pineapple.
Ice cream is as tasty as chicken,
Raspberries are like strawberries,
Apples are as juicy as blackcurrants,
Cookies are as mouth-watering as lemon,
Garlic bread is like pizza.

Tony Dowie (7)
Royston Primary School, London

Anxiety

Anxiety is dark blue like worries at the back of your head.
Anxiety looks like evil spirits.
Anxiety smells like burnt bread.
Anxiety is three-day rotten milk.
Anxiety feels like water just slipping from your hand.
Anxiety is an out of tune guitar string.
It reminds me of when my mum is as late as a bat getting home.

Fergus O'Loan (9)
St Elizabeth's Catholic Primary School, Richmond

Generosity

Generosity is pink like roses in a garden blowing quietly in the wind.
Generosity looks like things that are kind, roses, cats and little
children sharing.
Generosity smells like scents from a flower smelling as beautiful
as it looks.
Generosity feels all fluffy and cuddly just like a pillow ready for use.
Generosity sounds like the humming of birds.
Generosity tastes like marshmallows and hot chocolate, extremely
tasty and delicious.
Generosity reminds me of when I have been given something nice.

Honor Rudd (9)
St Elizabeth's Catholic Primary School, Richmond

Achievement

Achievement is golden like a medal shining in the sunlight.
Achievement sounds like the clapping of hands.
Achievement smells like something new.
Achievement looks like smiling faces.
Achievement tastes of red, ripe apples.
Achievement is the feeling of doing something you haven't
done before.
It reminds me of when I go to the head teacher for brilliant work.

Emily Wenman (9)
St Elizabeth's Catholic Primary School, Richmond

Responsibility

Responsibility is yellow like the candle burning bright.
It looks like being serious,
It smells like fresh air,
It tastes as nice as a cake,
It feels nice to be trusted.
It reminds me of when I am trusted.

George Pearce (9)
St Elizabeth's Catholic Primary School, Richmond

Excitement

Excitement is orange like the bright sun shining in the clear
summer sky.
It looks like a diamond beginning to shine.
It smells like a bright fire beginning to burn brightly.
It sounds like a twinkle of a star in the dark night sky.
Excitement feels like a quiet drum starting to beat.
It tastes of an orange just picked from a tree.
It reminds me of when I eat juicy oranges just picked by my
Italian uncle!

Elena Garitta (9)
St Elizabeth's Catholic Primary School, Richmond

Freedom

Freedom is blue, like the clear sky with birds flying freely.
Freedom looks like a bird soaring in the sky.
Freedom smells like fresh green grass.
Freedom tastes like red, juicy apples.
Freedom feels like fresh air.
Freedom sounds like a thousand bells ringing.
It reminds me of when my summer holidays start!

Alessandra Whelan Merediz (9)
St Elizabeth's Catholic Primary School, Richmond

Kindness

Kindness is light pink like flamingos swimming in the sea!
Kindness looks like people holding hands and sharing.
Kindness smells like love in the air.
Kindness tastes like sweet lollipops!
Kindness feels like happy moments.
Kindness sounds like birds tweeting in the air.
Kindness reminds me of when I play with my friends.

Driéla Pereira Collins (9)
St Elizabeth's Catholic Primary School, Richmond

Responsibility

Responsibility is bright purple like the clouds in the sky at sunrise.
It is sharing and caring and looking after what is yours.
It looks so beautiful.
It smells like lavender in a flower garden.
It tastes like berries recently picked.
It feels like you have just done something so great.
It sounds like birds chirping as the clouds come up at sunrise and
go down at sunset.
It reminds me of when I am good and helping.
It is as happy as a smile
And as hard-working as a servant.

Lara Rogers (10)
St Elizabeth's Catholic Primary School, Richmond

Courage

Courage is golden like the sun burning bright.
Courage looks like a lion as brave as a bear.
Courage smells like a brave man.
Courage tastes like bread that belongs to a brave creature.
Courage feels like a hairy lion that is about to do battle.
Courage smells of a roar.
It reminds me of when a lion is about to kill an animal that is
bigger than it.

Matthew Ilube (9)
St Elizabeth's Catholic Primary School, Richmond

Gratefulness

Gratefulness is blue like the sky at dawn,
It smells like the fresh air at night.
It tastes like ginger beer with the fizz.
It feels good inside.
It sounds like a dog barking.
It reminds me of good times.

Samuel MacKenzie (9)
St Elizabeth's Catholic Primary School, Richmond

Jealousy

Jealousy is navy like the gloomy, dull tunnel in the winter.
Jealousy looks like bullies at dark.
Jealousy smells like rotten eggs.
The sound of jealousy is a scream calling for help.
Jealousy tastes like cold, old Brussels sprouts.
The feel of jealousy is like a rock being thrown at me repeatedly.
It reminds me of when I see people with cold hearts.

Polly White (10)
St Elizabeth's Catholic Primary School, Richmond

Jealousy

Jealousy is grey like thunder on a pouring night.
Jealousy tastes like rotten food.
Jealousy feels like something stuck inside.
Jealousy looks like a grey sky.
Jealousy sounds like hailstones hitting the ground.
It reminds me of when I was jealous of one of my friends.

Claudia Barron (10)
St Elizabeth's Catholic Primary School, Richmond

Happiness

Happiness is yellow like the sun on a summer's day.
Happiness is like the sunshine shining.
It feels like the yellow sunshine.
Happiness sounds like fun.

Kamil Suckocki (9)
St Elizabeth's Catholic Primary School, Richmond

Sweety Sweets

I love sweets,
I want them every day,
I know they are not good for me,
But I eat them anyway.

My favourites are fruit gums,
They re juicy and sweet,
There are lots of different flavours,
They are all so nice to eat.

There are lots of different flavours,
My favourite one is red,
When all the reds are gone,
I stumble off to bed.

'You know you shouldn't eat them,'
Say the voices in my head,
But I always make sure my teeth are cleaned
Before I go to bed.

Lauren Flynn (10)
St Elizabeth's Catholic Primary School, Richmond

On A Beach

On a beach so far away,
Where ladies' bonnets would blow away,
The little men so merry,
Their little noses just like a cherry,
Their plump, rosy cheeks as pink as blossom,
Would light up the world for a possum.
Now all these characters that you've just heard
Look up to the face of one little bird!

Lauren Donaldson (9)
St Elizabeth's Catholic Primary School, Richmond

Day And Night

The beautiful sun
Is a fire
Which burns all day and
Goes out at night.
It's just like a
Candle burning bright.

The moon takes over
When night appears.
It's a torch in
The night,
Like coal.

Stars join the moon
And together they make
A beautiful light.
They look like lots of white roses
Shining in the night.

Raquel Traseira Pedraz (9)
St Elizabeth's Catholic Primary School, Richmond

Patience

Patience is white like a flying dove.
It looks like a cloud floating by.
It smells of roses and freshly-cut grass.
It tastes like strawberries and cream.
The sound of patience is laughing voices.
The feel of patience is warm and happy.
It reminds me of when I am looking forward
To something so good I don't want it to end.

Thalia Kent-Egan (9)
St Elizabeth's Catholic Primary School, Richmond

Relief

Relief is all colours, like the sun setting
And the moon and stars shining and sparkling in the moonlight.
Relief smells like the fresh air in the forest
On a glorious spring night.
It sounds like a little bird calling in a tree
Like it wants to be your friend.
Relief is like putting your finger in a stream
While it runs by and falls down a waterfall
Like it has something to send.
Relief reminds me of happiness
That sways around in the wind and gives you joy.

Conor O'Hara (9)
St Elizabeth's Catholic Primary School, Richmond

Sadness

Sadness is clear blue like the ocean on a summer's day.
Sadness sounds like the coast.
Sadness hurts the most.
Sadness feels like you've broken in half.
You can't cure sadness with a nice hot bath.
Sadness tastes like something biting your tongue.
You can't cure sadness with a sweet, juicy bun.
The only cure for sadness is your mum!

Millie Brogden (9)
St Elizabeth's Catholic Primary School, Richmond

Anger

Anger is black like the dark night sky.
It looks like red faces
And smells like smoke out of ears.
It feels like a jealousy bud inside you
And sounds like heavy breath in your face.
It reminds me of when my sister annoys me.

Daniel O'Sullivan (9)
St Elizabeth's Catholic Primary School, Richmond

Fear

Fear is a twirling purple like spiders in a misty, dark forest.
It looks like a big tornado spinning round and round,
Making me dizzier and dizzier every second.
Fear smells like burnt toast on rainy mornings.
It tastes like biting a mint and breaking a tooth.
Fear feels like a snake twisting and turning up my leg.
It sounds like a howling werewolf at midnight.
It reminds me of when I'm in bed
And the curtains are blowing and the floorboards are creaking.

Katie Duffy (10)
St Elizabeth's Catholic Primary School, Richmond

Happiness

Happiness is yellow like the sun shining down on everyone.
Happiness looks light, shiny and bright.
Happiness smells like bread, fresh and home-made, not a tinge
of red.
Happiness tastes sweet, sweet as the birds that tweet.
Happiness feels high, like you're floating in the sky.
Happiness sounds like birds tweeting a song,
When you wish each note to last very long.
It reminds me of my birthdays.

Antonia Ruddle (9)
St Elizabeth's Catholic Primary School, Richmond

Freedom

Freedom is green like beautiful grass.
It smells just like the times I go in the bath.
It feels like a lovely river running by.
It sounds like my favourite music.
It reminds me of when I leave school every day.

Hamish Macleod (9)
St Elizabeth's Catholic Primary School, Richmond

Hope

Hope is violet like a disco light shining bright.
Hope smells like fresh air.
Hope tastes like fresh apple juice.
Hope feels like happiness and joy.
It sounds like a thousand bells ringing.
It reminds me of when I want something to happen.

Archie Adams (9)
St Elizabeth's Catholic Primary School, Richmond

Autumn - Haiku

Leaves are falling down,
Colours falling to the ground,
Purple, green and brown.

Esme Rogers (8)
St Elizabeth's Catholic Primary School, Richmond

Faith

Faith is blue, it looks like the sky.
Faith feels like happiness, like people being kind to each other.
Faith tastes like a fresh apple.
Faith smells like an orange.
Faith reminds me of when I pray.

Sebastien Byrnes Soler (9)
St Elizabeth's Catholic Primary School, Richmond

Autumn Leaves - Haiku

Autumn is here now,
Say goodbye to summertime,
Crunchy leaves falling.

Henry Sempers-Spangenberg (8)
St Elizabeth's Catholic Primary School, Richmond

Autumn - Haiku

Leaves are falling down,
Red, green, orange and yellow,
It is autumn now.

Jasmine Rienecker (8)
St Elizabeth's Catholic Primary School, Richmond

The Leaves - Haiku

Goodbye to summer
Autumn is coming so quick
Leaves are falling down.

Sean Mackenzie (8)
St Elizabeth's Catholic Primary School, Richmond

Hedgehogs In Autumn - Haiku

The flowers have died,
Hedgehogs are under the leaves,
Winter is coming.

Thomas Pongrácz (8)
St Elizabeth's Catholic Primary School, Richmond

Hello Autumn - Haiku

Leaves are falling down,
Yellow, red, orange and brown.
Goodbye summer sounds.

Jack Sice (9)
St Elizabeth's Catholic Primary School, Richmond

Autumn Has Come Again - Haiku

The leaves are rustling,
Leaves are brown and red and gold,
Hedgehogs are asleep.

Joseph Sexton (9)
St Elizabeth's Catholic Primary School, Richmond

Sunset On The Trees - Haiku

Red, brown, golden leaves.
Late leaves swinging off the trees.
Leaves munching, crunching.

Thomas Ridley (9)
St Elizabeth's Catholic Primary School, Richmond

Say Goodbye Summer - Haiku

Goodbye to summer,
Please do not leave us today,
Winter is coming.

Ellie Reynolds (8)
St Elizabeth's Catholic Primary School, Richmond

Autumn Time - Haiku

Almost Christmastime,
Leaves are starting to fall down.
I will miss summer.

Georgina Brogden (8)
St Elizabeth's Catholic Primary School, Richmond

Autumn - Haiku

Hello to autumn,
The cool breeze blows leaves from trees.
Goodbye to autumn.

Rob Postle (8)
St Elizabeth's Catholic Primary School, Richmond

Autumn - Haiku

Leaves are falling down
And autumn is really fun.
The birds are flying.

Freddie Billinge (8)
St Elizabeth's Catholic Primary School, Richmond

Autumn Leaves - Haiku

Red, yellow and blue,
Every leaf has a colour
And you have one too.

Michael Udemba (8)
St Elizabeth's Catholic Primary School, Richmond

Autumn Leaves - Haiku

Play with leaves all day,
Leaves are flying all day long,
Red, green, orange, brown.

Madeleine Wenman (8)
St Elizabeth's Catholic Primary School, Richmond

Say Hello To Autumn - Haiku

Hello to autumn,
Brown, crunchy leaves are falling.
Breezes blowing around.

Tara Dilley (8)
St Elizabeth's Catholic Primary School, Richmond

The Autumn Leaves - Haiku

Maroon-coloured leaves,
Autumn is here, have no fear.
Take a look around.

Colette Staveley (8)
St Elizabeth's Catholic Primary School, Richmond

Leaves Are All Around - Haiku

Leaves are all around,
Falling till they touch the ground,
Not making a sound.

Georgia Hopley (8)
St Elizabeth's Catholic Primary School, Richmond

Colours - Haiku

Autumn is here now,
Purple, brown, red and yellow,
Winter is coming.

Meredith Webb (8)
St Elizabeth's Catholic Primary School, Richmond

Autumn

The leaves are turning red and yellow like a beautiful sunset.
They're turning and swirling and falling, like a ballerina dancer.
The trees are swaying and groaning in the changing wind
Because it's turning . . . turning . . . turning
Into an autumn spring.

The children are trudging in anoraks, with their hoods up high.
There are no smiles now because they're all shy.
Autumn and winter are coming to pay a small visit,
But they haven't seen them for ages . . . ages . . . ages,
But now summer's through.

Rachel Gracie Cheng (11)
St Elizabeth's Catholic Primary School, Richmond

My Autumn Poem - Haiku

Falling leaves are brown,
The cool breeze is coming now.
Goodbye to summer.

Jim Moffat (8)
St Elizabeth's Catholic Primary School, Richmond

Autumn Is Here - Haiku

Autumn is here now,
Trees with leaves begin to fall,
Sun sets in the sky.

Elizabeth Tracey (8)
St Elizabeth's Catholic Primary School, Richmond

The Eyes Have It

They say the eyes are the window to the soul
So open the shutter and make me whole
When I look I see the fear
All I want is to hold you near

I see you in the distance
Not sure if I should take a chance
Give it all up for you
Or begin again and start anew

No more revenge, no more doubt
I'm not strong enough for another bout
Forgive and forget, put hate out of my mind
An eye for an eye makes the whole world blind.

Millie Melvin (10)
St Elizabeth's Catholic Primary School, Richmond

Autumn

Children are playing with conkers,
While parents are going bonkers.
Garden pubs are closing down,
Summer is gone and autumn is here now.

The weather isn't warm any more,
Everything I hold
Is always very cold.

The days are not as long as they used to be.
I can still see myself swimming in the sea
And all my friends talking to me.

Valeria Gavazzeni (10)
St Elizabeth's Catholic Primary School, Richmond

The Sweet Sweets Poem

This is the sweet poem, the poem with lots of sweets!
Polos so minty they sting on your tongue,
Jelly that wobbles, full of fun,
Caramel so creamy and very gooey,
But if left in the fridge it's very chewy.
Some sweets are fizzy and make you go whizzy,
Some are just nice
And some made of rice.
I like sweets a lot,
Though my dentist says no,
But what does she know?
She only eats casserole!

Hannah Sturton (10)
St Elizabeth's Catholic Primary School, Richmond

Kallum's Poem

Eleven players on a team,
They play on a pitch that is the colour green.
They run up the pitch
While passing to one another,
It's more for dads and not for mothers.
The ref is there to make it fair,
So they don't kick or punch
Or pull their hair.
And that's the game you hear about,
But watch out for the fans
Because they scream and shout!

Kallum Parker-Andrew (11)
St Elizabeth's Catholic Primary School, Richmond

A Day At Anfield

It was when I went to Anfield
That I changed my team today,
Sitting on those plastic chairs
Is where my dignity lay.

The scent of cut grass surrounded us
As the players came out to play,
The stadium lights shone on the grass
So we could watch the game today.

A cup match filled with game
As the two teams fought
Hard tackles and hard shots,
You couldn't see much more,

At half-time it was 2-2,
Gerrard and Dirk Kuyt,
Shorey made the fourth goal,
It ended in a draw.

The second half began,
The game was up in flames,
As the Liverpool badge was shaking,
As Liverpool scored again.

The Liverpool game was 3-2,
When someone scored again,
This time it wasn't Liverpool,
This time it was Reading.

The game had nearly ended
When Liverpool scored a fourth,
Alonso from a free kick
Drilled across the floor.

The final whistle blew,
The managers shook their hands,
The Liverpool fans were happy
As they didn't get what they planned.

The sky was filled with darkness
As the fans' heads were held up high,
The game was just amazing,
As for Anfield they said bye-bye.

Patrick Roberts (10)
St Elizabeth's Catholic Primary School, Richmond

Maradona, Maradona!

Maradona, Maradona, don't you threat,
Punch that ball into the net.
Rooney, Rooney, don't be thick,
'Cause then you can score a hat-trick!
Neville, Neville be like Cole
So that you can score a goal!
Terry, Terry tick the ball on its side,
But don't get it offside!
Beckham, Beckham get sick,
But just after you score a free kick!
Ferguson, Ferguson eat your gum
While you watch your favourite chum!
Van Der Sar, Van Der Sar
We all know that you can go far!
Pele, Pele, do some skills,
Just make sure you pay your bills!
Ronaldo, Ronaldo just be cool,
But just make sure you're not a fool!
Lampard, Lampard get that ball,
Don't wait for a call.

Liam Maher (10)
St Elizabeth's Catholic Primary School, Richmond

The Sun

As I lie in bed in the early hours,
It has just gone five on the bedside clock,
The sun peeping through my childish curtains,
Lighting the gold metal on my bedroom door lock.

I look up at the sky, the sun smiling down,
But I am not smiling as school lies ahead.
The lessons, the teachers, the bully, the boredom,
My first day at big school fills me with dread.

I ignore my teacher as she yaps on about fractions,
By staring out of the window at the carefree sun.
Oh how I wish I was anywhere but here,
Out with my old friends and having some fun.

Sitting by myself in the bright sunlight,
Opening my lunch box and feeling blue,
Some girls come towards me and I fear the worst,
But they just want to sit in the sun too!

As I look at the sun at the end of the day,
Absent-mindedly making my way home alone,
Who should I meet but the girls who love sunshine.
We laugh and joke all the way home.

The sun is long gone as I lie in my bed,
Thinking to myself about the day that is done,
The friends that I made, the laughs that we had,
But above all, my constant companion, the sun.

Jennifer Tracey (10)
St Elizabeth's Catholic Primary School, Richmond

Christmas Poem

Christmas is coming and the ducks are being fed,
Please thank Jesus before you go to bed.
Don't be greedy and wish for more than love,
Or Jesus won't like it looking down from up above.

Jesus the saviour of all mankind is coming,
He helps us to pray and love God,
Teaching us different things wise and wonderful.

Christmas is coming and the ducks are being fed,
Please thank Jesus before you go to bed.
Don't be greedy and wish for more than love,
Or Jesus won't like it looking down from up above.

Spare a prayer for the poor and needy,
Spare a prayer for the homeless and lonely,
Think of those who don't have as much as us.

Christmas is coming and the ducks are being fed,
Please thank Jesus before you go to bed.
Don't be greedy and wish for more than love,
Or Jesus won't like it looking down from up above.

Claire O'Donoghue (10)
St Elizabeth's Catholic Primary School, Richmond

If I Were A Tree . . .

I've often wondered how it would be
To be as tall as a tree
Looking over commons and parks
Providing a home for all the larks
Squirrels and insects live there too
Busy all day doing the things they do
My leaves falling to the ground
Nearly without making a sound
Until I've made a carpet below
Ready to greet the winter snow.

Nicolas Daborn (10)
St Elizabeth's Catholic Primary School, Richmond

Seaside

Sea

The cold splash of the sea on your face,
Slithery seaweed slimy on your feet
And sparkly waves glistering towards you.

Sand

When your feet touch the sand
It makes you feel happy.
Inside it's so smooth, it makes you want to lie down.

Speedboats

A speedboat goes as fast as a Lamborghini
And leaves waves behind that sparkle
In the light of the sun.

Fish

The slithery fish in the glistening sea
That swim like dolphins splashing about in the sea.

Relaxing

You relax on the beach by lying down
On the nice soft sand, looking at the sight of the sea.

Ben Townsend (9) & Joshua Ballard (10)
St James CE Primary School, Hanney

At The Fairground

A roller coaster swirls and curls in different ways,
Like a boat on a stormy sea.
The roller coaster sometimes goes
Down into a dive like you and me.

When you eat candyfloss it feels like
A spider has spun a web in your mouth.
It melts and melts until it's gone,
Like ice cream with the help of the sun.

Katie Burge & Alison Downes (9)
St James CE Primary School, Hanney

The Seaside

The seaside is like a pool of excitement,
Waiting for everyone to come.
There are seagulls and shells,
But don't forget the salty smells.
There are also the sandy shores.

The slippery, slimy seaweed
Ripples in the roaring white waves
As the microscopic creatures
Crawl up the salty reefs.

The foaming waves
Brush against the undiscovered,
Making them scurry
For cover.

The surfboard shimmers
As the white waves crash
Against the swift surfer
Gliding across the roaring ocean.

Flo Myerscough-Harris & Paige Topley (10)
St James CE Primary School, Hanney

A Marine Journey

The sea rushes into rock pools flooding them
With salty water surprising creatures all around.
All white and frothy like a pint of lager.

Sloppy, slush, tasty too!
And it melts like a snowman on a sunny day.

I felt hot and bothered, the sun was beating down on me
Like a million bees stinging me everywhere.

It smelt of sweaty people, suncream and the sweet smell
Of the sea breeze air and the greasy fish and chips.

I could feel the rough, crunchy sand between my toes
And the sloppy, melted ice cream slithering down the cone.

Michael Ledbury (9) & Aaron Tidmus (10)
St James CE Primary School, Hanney

A Trip To The Seaside

You can smell the scent of suntan lotion
On sunbathers slowly roasting in the sun,
And as you walk along the rocks you can feel
The slimy texture of the slippery seaweed
Floating to and fro on the shallow shores.

You can hear the squelch of seaweed
As you tiptoe nimbly through it.
You can also hear all the children laughing and screaming
Like a herd of elephants stomping, non-stop!

You can see a sea of striped deckchairs
With bright blue windbreaks around them.
You can also see lots of little children
Making sandcastles with their friends.
All their fun will never end.

Do not forget the taste at the seaside.
You can taste the gritty sand in your mouth
As it makes you tingle all over.

Sophie Jeffreys & Corissa Belprez (10)
St James CE Primary School, Hanney

Holiday In France

Excitement on the ferry as it approaches the docks.
The car comes off, we're finally on holiday.

The strong must of the ruby-red wine rose from the glass
Filling the air with a fruity fragrance.
The white wine sparkled like a diamond in the evening light.
Pastry crumbles in your mouth with a rich buttery flavour.
Fillings like chocolate make you smile.

Touching the cold stone of the church brings shivers to your spine.
The warm feeling of the church pews.

Walking into the bustling markets giving off a roar of shouts,
As the stench of food hits you into a mirage of colours.

Sam Jarman & Edward Evans (10)
St James CE Primary School, Hanney

Lizard

Lizard

The lizard's stealthy footsteps
Quickly picked up as it
Chased its lively prey.

Coral

With its charming radiant tinge
It sways side to side like
The Mexican wave at a football match.

Waves

They reflect blurry images of the boats
As they shimmer in the sunset.

Corey Roberts & Harrison Crick (10)
St James CE Primary School, Hanney

Autumn

Raindrops falling from a dripping sponge cloud,
Creeping down the windowpanes.
Bees rushing to get the last parcels of pollen.
Frost veiling the ground like an autumn bride.
Fat robins going shopping for worms.
The fierce wind pressing against our faces.
Green, spiky conker shells protecting the baby seed inside.
Animals going to bed and turning off the light
Ready for the following spring.

Connie Rogers & Sophie Constance (9)
St Peter's CE Primary School, Cassington

Autumn

Multicoloured leaves parachuting off the trees
As Wind whispers secrets to the birds
The sun is sitting on his cloudy, squishy sofa
Red Squirrel plays hide-and-seek
Busily hiding her winter supply of nuts.

Burning leaves fill the air with a pungent smell
Stagnant water smells like a wet shaggy dog
Blackberry jam cooking on the stove
Smelling like sweet pear drops.

Litter being swept off the streets
Wind breathing its warm breath over us
Spiky little hedgehogs falling on our heads
Fireworks exploding in the autumn night's sky
Animals snoring in their hibernation bed.

Yummy hot chocolate warming up your cold hands
The heat of the bonfire warming up your face
Warm breath making misty clouds
Snuggling up in your warm duvet.

Ben Copelin, Chloe Constance, Fern Hinton (9),
Amber Brixton & Adam Langdon (10)
St Peter's CE Primary School, Cassington

My Autumn

Glistening, polished acorns dropping from up high,
Migrating birds turn into black specks
In the orange and yellow sky
As they leave for a warmer climate.
Children shouting trick or treat
As they run from door to door.
Raindrops racing down the windows
As the golden sun goes into hiding.

Bonnie Harvey (9)
St Peter's CE Primary School, Cassington

Autumn Senses

Scarlet leaves cover the ground,
Wind is blowing all around.
Bonfire Night with big bangs,
Hallowe'en with vampires' fangs.

Crackling leaves everywhere,
On the ground and in the air.
Snapping twigs off the trees,
We can break them, you and me.

Sweet aroma of apple pies,
Rising up into the skies.
Chestnuts cooking on the stove,
Pleasant smells up your nose.

Conkers plummeting to the floor,
One by one, more and more.
Spiky shells pricking your fingers,
Cracking open as they fall.

Conor Byles (9) & Steve Wright (10)
St Peter's CE Primary School, Cassington

Lovely Autumn

Leaves in their golden and rouge dresses
Dance in the cool, fresh breeze.
Bonfires being lit, smoke rising into the sky,
Misty gardens covered in a blanket of snow,
Looking like they are ready for bed.
Hedgehogs snuggling in a bed of leaves,
Foxes creeping along frosty fields foraging for their food,
Squirrels scuttling up oak trees, hiding their winter store,
Trees shaking off their summer clothes.
The smell of freshly-cut grass makes your nostrils tingle.
The wafting blackberry and apple crumble
Mixing with the foul odours of fertilizers
As farmers plough their fields.
The aroma of the country.

Hannah Griggs & Victoria Partridge (10)
St Peter's CE Primary School, Cassington

An Autumn Day

The gusty wind chasing crimson and ochre leaves
Across the frostbitten ground.
Mice and squirrels scavenging for a last minute supply of food.
A smell of hot chocolate and apple pie filling the air.
Armies of geese shouting orders at each other
Before beginning their long journey.
Conkers jumping off trees in their spiky green armour.
Hedgehogs snuggled up under a soft duvet of moss
Fall into a deep sleep.
Sparkling cobwebs like lace decorating the grass.
Rosy-red berries standing alone on bare bushes.
A whispering breeze lifting the bonfire's
Curly smoke up into the night sky.
Carpets of cheerful umbrellas sheltering
The busy city from the silver rain.
Mother Nature switches off the light
At the end of another autumn day.

Lydia Johnston (9) & Beatrice Taylor (10)
St Peter's CE Primary School, Cassington

Autumn Leaves

Leaves rustling on the trees,
Bonfires crackling, burning all the fallen leaves.

The leaves have now changed colour from green to orange to red,
The daylight is getting shorter, I will soon be in my bed.

The weather's getting colder now,
The smoke from the bonfire, what a smell!

Luke Hoesli (9)
St Peter's CE Primary School, Cassington

Autumn Breeze!

The ashy smell of smoky bonfires tickling our noses.
Pictures of November appear in the spitting flames
As they consume the end of summer.

Conkers and acorns falling create the sound of a strike
On a drum as they collide with the ground.

The crimson and golden-brown leaves samba-ing
Dramatically as they rush to the grassy floor.

The embarrassed cherry blush of the early sunset sky,
Gently closing the day.

A jamboree of autumn fruits, bursting blackberries,
Juicy red currants and plump blueberries,
Tumbling like acrobats into a crusty pie.

Jack Frost gripping the windowpane
While the illuminating moon gives the look
Of snow-covered ground, bringing whispers of Christmas.

Francesca Lovell (9) & Grace Brixton (10)
St Peter's CE Primary School, Cassington

Ocean

White waves captured by the frightful wind,
It's a bath for the world.
The sun is coming out to cover the frosty sea,
Beaming down and standing proud.
Water lashing against the rocks,
It's making the roaring sound.
The moon shines over the sea.
The big blue blanket is asleep,
It is still and quiet.

Sophie Purdy (10)
Sparrow Farm Community Junior School, Stoneleigh

The Deep Blue

Water, water everywhere,
Wherever you look,
Wherever you stare,
It's over here,
It's over there.
Water, water everywhere.
As the water splashes down to the ground,
You can hear it all around.
Very cold in the deep blue,
Especially the mist at the bottom too.
On the warm tropical beach,
That's where I lay.
I might jump in another day,
But definitely not today.
Water, water everywhere,
Wherever you look,
Wherever you stare,
It's over here,
It's over there.
Water, water everywhere.

Hollie Drewett (10)
Sparrow Farm Community Junior School, Stoneleigh

Water

The water looked as hot as a kettle boiling,
The reflection was blinding.
The water smelt of salt.
The waves were destroying the rocks.
The sea is a giant bath.
The drip-drop of water from your tap,
As blue as Chelsea's football kit.
The sound of the wind blowing across the sea,
Crash! Deafening you.
It is as loud as a piano crashing on the floor.
Water is everything.

Jordan Heavens (10)
Sparrow Farm Community Junior School, Stoneleigh

The Sea

The sea is a fluffy cloud
Shimmering in the light.
The waves are roaring lions.
It's an inspirational sight.

The waterfall is crashing down
Into the bright blue sea,
And splashing up at the edges,
Occasionally wetting me.

The river is beautiful,
It makes a sensational sound,
Bubbling and gurgling.
This is a remarkable place
That someone has found!

Anna Seddon (10)
Sparrow Farm Community Junior School, Stoneleigh

Waterfall

A waterfall skimming against rocks,
Shining like a mirror,
As blue as the sky,
Shimmering like silver hair,
Zooming down the mountainside
Like a person on a roller coaster,
Then splashing at the bottom.
The noise is an ear-piercing *boom*.

Piers Reucroft (10)
Sparrow Farm Community Junior School, Stoneleigh

A Calm Sea

As the gentle tide ebbs and flows,
The massive stones are still,
Not moving an inch.
The time goes by
And the big stones get smaller and smaller.
Although the little ones are washed away,
They will be on another beach some day
To start a new stone age.
Tiny little sea creatures
Swim about happily.
They know the sea is calm
So they've nothing to fear in this calm and gentle sea.
This sea is friendly,
This sea is calm.

Brandon Robins (10)
Sparrow Farm Community Junior School, Stoneleigh

Untitled

The water is like a diamond's edge.
The water is a typhoon spinning wildly.
Shining blue water crashing to the rocks below.
The bubbling water is like a mirror.
The water is a single emerald, coloured a pretty blue-green.
A sapphire is the water's glimmer.
The speeding water is slashing through rocks.

Owen Chan (10)
Sparrow Farm Community Junior School, Stoneleigh

Calm Sea

The sea gives a gentle splash,
Makes a crash as quiet as a mouse.
A little wave hits a rock,
Drops slowly, hits the soft, smooth sand.
The warm yellow sun shines on the quiet blue sea.
All you can hear is the waves gently crashing.
You can feel little drops hit your face.
You can taste the salty water.
You can see the seaweed on the slippery, shiny rocks.
The only noise you can hear is the birds
Slowly flying past.
The sea is so calm and quiet.

Nicki Erodotou (10)
Sparrow Farm Community Junior School, Stoneleigh

Niagara

A mighty warrior,
Destroys everything in its path.
Phenomenal sound
Like a mighty lion's roar.
Crystals gracefully
Falling off a cliff.
Suicidal jump,
To brave water droplets,
So wildly fast
Like a cheetah running off a wall.

Alfie Stockwell (11)
Sparrow Farm Community Junior School, Stoneleigh

Waterfall

Water like a roller coaster
Tumbling off the edge of the track.
The ear-piercing sound of a hungry pack of lions
Attacking their prey.
A gigantic essence of bubble bath,
Floating up into the foggy air.
A rumbling giant ready to eat.
The reflecting light of the blinding sun
On the clear blue sea.

Robert Mutch (10)
Sparrow Farm Community Junior School, Stoneleigh

H₂O

A waterfall is like a hot, bubbly bath,
With a little rubber duck.

The sea sounds like a hamster drinking its water.
A waterfall is like a blue blanket wrapping around the world.

The sea is sparkly and bright,
Like a sunset.

Trinidad Challenger (10)
Sparrow Farm Community Junior School, Stoneleigh

Waterfall

A waterfall goes down a slide as fast as a roller coaster.
Underneath the big waterfall slide there is
Nice hot water covered in white, fluffy foam.
The rocks get a shower when they
Get soaked by the waterfall.
The sound is as loud as a trumpet
Being blown in your ear.

Thanzil Uddin (10)
Sparrow Farm Community Junior School, Stoneleigh

The Waterfall

Like an endless slide slipping to the floor,
Glimmering sun shining over a pool of light,
A bubble bath boiling below,
The top is calm and slow like a turtle,
Then crashing down to the rocks below.

Clara Gibson (10)
Sparrow Farm Community Junior School, Stoneleigh

Water

W aterfall's crashing down
A s fast as it possibly can.
T he sea is like a blue blanket covering the Earth.
E ar-splitting noise, louder than the sonic boom.
R emarkable views of the misty water spraying up.

Sam Jenkins (10)
Sparrow Farm Community Junior School, Stoneleigh

The Crashing Waterfall

The water falling down to the sea,
Rushing like a running race,
Splashing drops, diving to smack the rocks,
Water crashing on my head,
Sounding like an earthquake coming.

Hollie Egremont (11)
Sparrow Farm Community Junior School, Stoneleigh

At The Waterfall

The silent water was trickling down the sparkling stream.
Suddenly, *crash!* The dazzling water drifts down
And nearly over the edge of the bumpy cliff.
Then again down another waterfall and *swoosh* the waves went,
And the glamorous water strikes against the rough, sharp rocks.
The silky soft water feels like a blanket of snow.
You can see the blue sky and birds circling the water.
You can smell the sweet, salty, water, sweeping and dazzling.
You can hear the crashing of the waves striking
On the rough, ruined rocks and weeping over the cliff.
You can taste the ice cream from the stall by the cliff.

Alainna Chambers (10)
Sparrow Farm Community Junior School, Stoneleigh

The Amazing Waterfall

Pure, pearl-like water suddenly falls and disappears,
Twisting around like a tornado, covering the air with bubbles.
White foam explodes like galloping white horses out of control!

Shimmering, clear, ear-piercing,
Frothy bubbles floating above, filling the atmosphere.
Down it goes, trembling, lapping and lashing on slippery rocks!

Spinning around like the wheels of a car,
Slushy, bubbly water waiting to erupt.
Bits of rocks floating on top, spinning around and around.

Laxsica Ranjan (11)
Sparrow Farm Community Junior School, Stoneleigh

Waterfalls

Waterfalls sound like a hammer banging in nails.
Waterfalls can run slow as snails.

Waterfalls glitter like fancy jewels.
Waterfalls don't obey the rules.

Waterfalls are as fast as cheetahs.
Waterfalls are special features.

Waterfalls sound like a librarian saying, *'Shh!'*
When waterfalls come to the end they go *whoosh!*

Charlotte Gosling (10)
Sparrow Farm Community Junior School, Stoneleigh

The Calm Sea

The sound of the rippling waves,
Seagulls squawking with their feathery brothers,
A blue sea shimmering like an expensive diamond,
And as silky as a soft silver cushion.

The sight of the clear blue sea reflecting off ancient cliffs,
A shimmering blanket hiding treasures below,
And in the distance you can see and hear dolphins,
The palm trees swaying in the calm, gentle wind.

Hannah Jarvis (10)
Sparrow Farm Community Junior School, Stoneleigh

Waterfall

Waterfall crashes against grey, dark rocks.
Waterfall making dancing reflections of the light,
Making little pictures on the beginning of the waterfall.
Waterfall, as blue as the sky.
Waterfall crashing against the rocks
Like a cheetah racing down a mountain.

Kayoon Kim (10)
Sparrow Farm Community Junior School, Stoneleigh

The Sea

It's early morning and the curving waves are crashing about.
The sun is shining down like the golden hair of Rapunzel.
I am just as happy as the scene around me.
There are playing children in the bashing waves,
So I say it's a happy place to be right beside the sea.
The day is coming to an end and I'm going to relax.
By the looks of things, so are the sun and sea.
The sun is setting
And the beautiful, crystal-clear water is now calm and quiet.
The water reflecting the glistening red sun makes an
                                    unbeatable scene.
I start a fire and guess what I see?
A dolphin,
A real, live dolphin.
It jumped out of the sparkling sapphire sea
And back into the mysterious pool of shimmering blue jewels.

Hannah Stone (10)
Sparrow Farm Community Junior School, Stoneleigh

Waterfalls

Water, water flying in the misty air,
The spray of the water is a white cloud in the blue sky.
Water rumbles down the lumpy rocks,
The light reflects onto the gushing waves.
Waves of water crashing onto the ground.
Water twisting and whirling like a tornado.

Hannah Rowe (10)
Sparrow Farm Community Junior School, Stoneleigh

A Water Fountain

There's a water fountain,
It trickles and splatters like a bit of white snow,
Touching the grass,
Plunging off and hitting the rocks.
Water of the water fountain falls on pebbles and explodes.
The water is like bullets dropping to the ground,
Going drip, drop, drip, drop.
The sound is like a lion roaring and shaking its mane,
And like an angry bull with fury,
Or a dog chasing a cat,
Thunder and lightning,
Like a bullet in the sky,
And a shark showing his white, crystal teeth,
Or a rocket zooming into space.

Loran Chambers (10)
Sparrow Farm Community Junior School, Stoneleigh

The Rushing Waterfall

The running water crashes down the sparkling waterfall,
Crashing like a child sliding down a slippery slope.
The bright sun reflects in the shimmering water like a mirror.
When you feel the water, you feel like a soft cushion.
You can also hear birds squawking
As they fly past the bubbling waterfall.

Sue-ling Chan-Wyles (10)
Sparrow Farm Community Junior School, Stoneleigh

Water

As the water crashes
And it also splashes,
The shiny sun beams
And makes the water gleam!

Sparkling sapphire sea
Glows constantly.
The sea is always shimmering,
Maybe even glimmering!

Sometimes pacing,
Sometimes racing,
The sea is sometimes low,
But nobody will ever know.

Tara Evlambiou (11)
Sparrow Farm Community Junior School, Stoneleigh

Water

Rushing like a Formula 1 car,
Shimmering in the gleaming sun.
Like a crystal-clear pool of blue,
Mile after mile of it,
Either crashing on rocks or
Standing as still as a statue.
Taking up all the space,
Growing faster than the human race.
There's no stopping this mighty power,
It's in a drink or in your shower,
It's everywhere!

Dominic Pencherz (10)
Sparrow Farm Community Junior School, Stoneleigh

Waterfalls

Water raging from the top
Comes gushing down,
Hitting the bottom with a splash
That erodes away silently.
The sound is so relaxing,
You could fall into a deep, deep, sleep.
The colour is magnificent.
Crystal-clear water shimmering in the sun.
At the bottom it's like a pool of froth . . .
Cold but luxurious . . .
No one knows what's underneath,
Evil or kindness.
Waterfalls.

Saffron Armstrong (10)
Sparrow Farm Community Junior School, Stoneleigh

The River

A river smashing on rocks,
Like a hurricane,
The storm hits the river,
The river splashes
Like a large rock falling from space.
Waves push the small boats
Backwards and forwards.
The river makes a horrible noise.

Edgar Gomes (11)
Sparrow Farm Community Junior School, Stoneleigh

The Falling Water

Its might,
It's falling and falling down
And smashing on the bottom of the floor.
You can't see anything
But the fluffy white . . .
Falling,
Falling,
Falling,
Falling,
Falling,
Falling,
Smashing!

Hayley Burden (10)
Sparrow Farm Community Junior School, Stoneleigh

The Mighty Waterfall

Bursting,
Raging,
The water's lashing,
Booming,
Crashing,
The water's frothing,
The wading water flashes by,
Cold air makes you shiver
By a river with a waterfall.

Luke Boulton (10)
Sparrow Farm Community Junior School, Stoneleigh

Water

Water, water everywhere,
Crashing on slippery rocks,
Sprinting off the edge like a motorbike.
At the bottom, a raging bubble bath,
Running rapids like a speeding train,
Smashing, crashing on sharp rocks.
Look at the dazzling view, glinting in my eye.
Ear-piercing water. Look out below!
It takes your breath away.
Water, water everywhere.

Billy Collier (10)
Sparrow Farm Community Junior School, Stoneleigh

Water

Water dripping from taps,
Roaring down as fast as light.
The water as cold as ice,
Like silver stripes of hair
Glistening in the bright sun,
Lashing against the rocks.
Water is full of energy.
Waterfalls shouting down.

Freddie Finnett (10)
Sparrow Farm Community Junior School, Stoneleigh

The Waterfall

Crystal-clear water rushes down,
Falling and exploding on the pointy black rocks.
Falling water is whipped up like milk in a whisk,
The crashing, smashing sound is deafening.

The water swarms with silver fish,
They twist and turn and race through the water.
They look like little muscles powering through the water,
Scales shimmering and shining in the bright sunlight.

Tropical birds dive into the water to catch their lunch,
Racing into the water as fast as a rocket.
The panicking fish try to swim away but the birds are too fast
                                          for them,
They fly like fighter jets when they soar through the air.

Water bubbles as it hits the rocky bottom.
The sharp, black rocks get covered in a beard of froth.
Water falls like water gushing from a tap,
Logs and plants that go down will be dragged to the bottom.

At the base there is a whirlpool
Looking like an underwater tornado,
Sucking up everything around it,
Like water going down a plughole.

Joshua Bull (11)
Sparrow Farm Community Junior School, Stoneleigh

Water

Like a monster roaring,
And the rain when it's pouring,
The huge sun makes it shimmer
And then it begins to glimmer.

Sun staring at the sparkling sea,
Whizzing about like a bee,
Every part like tiny blue stars,
Zooming around like some cars.

It's a late person rushing,
And a toilet flushing.
Looks like a beautiful crystal
And it's as loud as a pistol.

Come over here, you can listen,
Or we can just watch it glisten.
Look at it all gushing together,
I could just stand here and watch forever.

Going around the rocks crashing,
Tumbling over, splashing,
See all the waves
Racing about for days.

It does not go to bed at night,
It stays until the morning light.
The sun's beaming,
Watch it gleaming.

Chloe Hudson (10)
Sparrow Farm Community Junior School, Stoneleigh

Waterfalls!

W aterfall crumbling on the rocks
A crystal diamond shimmering
T housands of tears dripping
E xtraordinary blue blankets wrapping around me
R ushing and splashing on and on
F lashing and bellowing
A t last the tide is falling
L ashing and dashing, smaller and smaller
L eaping back to the sea
S eashells are seen again!

Oscar Stewart (10)
Sparrow Farm Community Junior School, Stoneleigh

Waterfall

Sparkling water smashing on the slippery rocks,
Like dangerous soldiers fighting.
Sun beaming on the clear blue water,
Water sparkling like a diamond.
Running water rushing down,
Like a tiger bounding down a long, steep hill.
An enormous slide.
Clouds of bubbles form below.

Callum McCarthy (11)
Sparrow Farm Community Junior School, Stoneleigh

Ocean

The ocean clashes against the rocks,
Bubbling all day, all night,
Dashing into a wave.
The ocean is as blue as Neptune,
Sparkles like a diamond.
The enjoyable sound is so calming,
So picturesque.

Curtis Gore (11)
Sparrow Farm Community Junior School, Stoneleigh

Rippling Waves

The sound of water makes me smile,
The home of crabs, fish and crocodiles.
Splish, splash, the rippling waves,
I like it when water cascades.
It shimmers, sparkles, I love it so,
The way the waves crash to and fro.

As blue as a gorgeous sapphire,
Oh no! The tide is getting higher,
So now it's time to go,
Time to pack away,
That's enough of the water
For one day!

Elena Hoskins (10)
Sparrow Farm Community Junior School, Stoneleigh

H_2O

The sunlight shines on the rippling lake
With light glistening off the fishes' scales.

Filling your eyes with tinkling topaz,
Repelling from the deep, deep down.

It is like the pouring of light blue slush,
Hitting the rocks and making mush.

Sparks flying off the shimmering downpour,
Crashing on the dark, dark rocks.

Gorgeous, gurgling H_2O,
Polluting water no, no, no.

Ethan Hogan (10)
Sparrow Farm Community Junior School, Stoneleigh

Waterfall

A cool, wet mist fills the chilly air.
Gently lapping against the rocks,
Gurgling and whirling,
Falling and dripping,
Making a screeching sound.

Splashing the ground below,
Reflecting back the blinding sunlight,
Rising in a drifting manner.
A resounding, ear-splitting noise,
Falling and dancing,
Gurgling and whirling,
Making a thundering sound.

Rushing down like a flash of lightning,
Shapeless and fearful,
Glistening and clear,
Sparkling in the sun.
Gurgling and whirling,
Falling and winding,
Will this ever end?

Phoebe Frewin (10)
Sparrow Farm Community Junior School, Stoneleigh

Waterfall

A waterfall is as blue as a sapphire.
When the water falls down,
And down and down and down,
You can hear the water crashing
Into the water below.
It sounds like a lion roaring in the jungle.
I sometimes wonder where the
Sparkling blue waterfall leads to.

Harrison Pike (11)
Sparrow Farm Community Junior School, Stoneleigh

Waterfalls

Water, water everywhere,
And not a drop to drink.
Water, water everywhere,
All gone down the sink.
Water is like fresh blood
Crashing through the mud.
It is screeching really loud,
Like people in a crowd.
Rocks are crashing,
Waves are bashing,
Water gleaming in your eyes,
Such a special surprise.
It sounds like a lion's roar.
A waterfall
Is never,
A bore!

Ryan Humphryes (10)
Sparrow Farm Community Junior School, Stoneleigh

The Waterfall

A waterfall is like water being chucked out of a skyscraper.
A waterfall makes dreadful sounds.
As the water hits the rocks, it starts to get out of bounds.
A waterfall is like someone sliding down the stairs.
A waterfall is a place for bears to eat.
A waterfall is a place of happiness.

Simon Hickman (10)
Sparrow Farm Community Junior School, Stoneleigh

A Waterfall

Water comes crashing down,
Thrashing against the groaning rocks,
Crashing and smashing water,
Misty water forming like a fire.

Ice-skaters skate across diamonds,
The waters are marathon runners running over the edge.

The sun is shining,
The water is glistening,
Water's smashing,
Water's thrashing.

A deafening thunder fills the air,
Rain comes lapping down with an ear-piercing boom.
This is an atmosphere for a waterfall!

William Cunningham (10)
Sparrow Farm Community Junior School, Stoneleigh

Waterfall

W atery substances rushing down rivers
A s blue as a butterfly's wings
T errific gurgles in the sea
E ager fish waiting for food
R eflects sunlight into your eyes
F rosty ice is glistening in the moonlight
A lot of pebbles moving into the sea
L et the spray rise
L et the waterfalls fall.

Michelle Sharpe (10)
Sparrow Farm Community Junior School, Stoneleigh

Rivers

Like a lazy dog basking
In the sunshine,
The water flows calmly
Down the stream,
Smashing at rocks,
Water going everywhere,
People screaming like roaring lions,
Babies crying everywhere.
Whooshing water dashing everywhere,
People going everywhere,
People getting wet everywhere,
Everyone shivering with towels on,
Everyone getting angry like furious dragons,
Bullets of water still going everywhere,
People still running everywhere.

Jed Thomas (11)
Sparrow Farm Community Junior School, Stoneleigh

Rivers

Like a lazy dog basking
In the sunshine,
The water flows calmly
Down the stream.
Crystals lying in the sun,
An Olympic runner in a race,
Rockets zooming into space,
Fireworks whooshing to the sky,
A boat bursting out of a chute,
As day turns to night,
Water flows calmly as it lies in bed.

Shehnaz Aziz (10)
Sparrow Farm Community Junior School, Stoneleigh

A Waterfall

Glistening, glowing
Like pretty jewels.

The water catches the light
Rainbow colours appear,
Reflecting its beauty on the rocks.

Like thousands of marching feet,
Like a mighty battle cry,
So the sound of the waterfall
Is carried across the land.

It overflows with beauty
And magnificence,
Dominating the land.

Its silver mane rushing into the depths of the river
Like a glistening blanket plunging down,
Eroding the outcrop of rocks below.

Precious Opara (10)
Sparrow Farm Community Junior School, Stoneleigh

Waterfall

A waterfall lurches on top of rocks,
Slowly it plunges itself over the edge.
It destroys anything in its path.
It glistens in the sun like a shining crystal
And comes down like racing cars.
It rumbles and roars when
Crashing against the rocks below,
Then slowly erodes into the gleaming river,
Fading in the distance.

Joseph Phillips (10)
Sparrow Farm Community Junior School, Stoneleigh

Waterfall

Water plunging, down and down,
Smashing rocks on the ground.
It's as loud as a tiger's roar,
Down it crashes, more and more.
Waterfall tumbling with loads of fear,
Louder and louder so everyone can hear.
Glistening and dazzling in the sun,
When it's calm it's much more fun.
Powerfully pulling the water down,
Down and down to the rough ground.
Curving in, out and around,
Crashing to the rocks with a mighty sound!

Chloe Kirby (11)
Sparrow Farm Community Junior School, Stoneleigh

Waterfall

W is for waves, crashing against the rocks.
A is for amazing as the water rushes down.
T is for trickling as it travels down the mountain.
E is for erosion as it's making its path.
R is for rocks standing in the way.
F is for fish as they play in the water.
A is for aquarium, full of tropical fishes.
L is for light shining on the water.
L is for lapping up and down the beach.

Georgina Baxter (10)
Sparrow Farm Community Junior School, Stoneleigh

Water

Water splashing,
Water crashing,
Water cold as ice.

Water lashing,
Water hurtling,
Water scattering like mice.

Water rippling,
Water gurgling,
Water shimmering in the sun.

Water tumbling,
Water splashing,
Water dazzling, oh what fun!

Water bubbling,
Water swishing,
Water glittering crystal-clear.

Water gushing,
Water roaring,
Water deep and full of fear.

Adam Levett & Zavien Smith (10)
Sparrow Farm Community Junior School, Stoneleigh

The Ocean

The water was sparkling like a sapphire,
It sounded happy as waves crashing peacefully together.
The ocean was blue and it was very beautiful,
It felt gentle like a baby's hand.
It looked as bubbly as a Jacuzzi.
The sun was shining on the ocean, it was lovely,
It was the most beautiful thing I've ever seen.
As the waves were beginning to crash together,
It made me feel sleepy.

Nayyara Malik (10)
Sparrow Farm Community Junior School, Stoneleigh

A Lovely Stream

A stream as harmless as cotton wool,
So exotic in a remote forest.
A dainty lady delicately walking,
As calm as a frozen statue.
No wasteland, no threat,
Running walls of silk whispering quietly.
Paradise for everyone,
As silent as the dead of night,
As relaxing as a gentle massage.

Myles Mitchell (10)
Sparrow Farm Community Junior School, Stoneleigh

Love Is

Love is a puppy in the park
Love is a baby in a buggy
Love is a kiss on the cheek
Love is a sunny day
Love is your dad picking you up
Love is your mum's voice telling you goodnight
Love isn't a lonely soul.

Lizzie Melville (9)
The Harrodian School, Barnes

Ode To A Tortoise

People think a tortoise is slow,
but I've watched one and this much I know.

They can run and fight and hide and chase
and sometimes they will even race
each other in the garden, over rocks.

So please don't ever mock
the tortoise; he is faster than you think.

Robert McBride (9)
The Harrodian School, Barnes

The Seasons

Ducks are laying eggs,
Swans are swimming in rivers,
This is the season, spring.
Daffodils growing, sun coming,
Bees buzzing, fish swimming,
This is an amazing season for the animals,
Bunnies are starting to hop, squirrels running up trees,
Plants are coming, ladybirds are flying and lots of birds are tweeting,
Rivers are shining, herons are ducking their beaks in ponds
And frogs are sitting on lily pads,
I love spring.

In the summer the pools get open,
In the summer the sky turns blue,
In the summer the sun comes out,
I love the summer, summer is great, summer is a thing I do not hate.
The heat on my face, sun loungers everywhere,
Turning brown, getting freckles, not a speckle of cold wind,
Flowers blooming, the grass is green, running about dipping in pools,
I love summer.

Autumn time is great, it is another thing I do not hate,
Find conkers off the trees and all the orange leaves,
Running around in muddy fields,
And walking in brown-coloured bushes and the September crushes,
I love autumn,

In the winter ice skating starts,
In the winter hot cocoa begins,
In the winter presents come back,
I love winter, Christmas time lights on the trees,
If you can, go skate on ice,
It is not dangerous but it is nice,
Skiing off hills near windmills,
Hot drinks, warm bread,
Cosy robes, what could be better than warmer toes?

Hot tea with lemon wedge,
It must be great with winter around,
I love winter.
All the warm stuff comes,
No more sunburnt tums.

Charlie Clark (9)
The Harrodian School, Barnes

Willow

I had a little dog,
She was so very fine,
Her coat was shiny tan and white
And we played together all the time.

When I was only little
She would walk beside my pram,
But as I grew much bigger
I would carry her in my hands.

She walked to school with me in the morning,
Her tail wagged when I got home each night,
We would spend our weekends together,
Never out of each other's sight.

She loved to chase rabbits
And splash in the waves on the beach by the sea,
And bark at the torchlight when I walked her in the evening,
It was forever fun just Willow and me.

Slowly she grew older
And our days running together in the woods grew few,
We buried her under the apple tree at the end of granny's garden
And I only hope she knew . . .

How very much I loved her
And how much I miss her too.

Sebastian Williams (10)
The Harrodian School, Barnes

Mad About Football

I'm mad about football
It's like Heaven to me
When I kick a ball
I'm soaring free.

The power in my foot
Takes me to another level
So whenever I shoot
The crowds just yell.

The strikers are afraid of me
Whenever I go near them
'Cause I blast them off their feet
And they go rolling down the street.

I'm mad about football
No mountains are too steep
I even kick a ball
When I'm in my sleep.

Max Cranmer (10)
The Harrodian School, Barnes

London

The hustle and bustle
The park with trees
The river that leads to the sea
Red buses shine in the sun
Black taxis work till the day is done
In the winter there are rinks full of ice
But the price is not so nice
In summer bees fill the trees
And the sun shines on all.

Anna Carruthers (9)
The Harrodian School, Barnes

I'm So Bored With Schoolwork

I'm so bored with schoolwork,
Nothing could be worse.
You get up in the morning,
Get dressed and go downstairs,
Eat up all your breakfast,
Brush your teeth and hair.
Then it's off for another day of torture,
French, English and maths,
Then hooray! It's break time,
You're free! You're free! You're free!
But after 20 minutes it's back in again.
The classroom's hot and stuffy
And oh no! The teacher is very grumpy,
Poor old me,
I'm so bored with schoolwork,
Nothing could be worse.

James Odgers (9)
The Harrodian School, Barnes

The Dragon

Its eyes were black as night.
Its roar was thunder.
Its skin was ice.
Its claws were sharp knives.
Its tail was fire.
Its fire was hot as the sun.
Its colour was black and red.
The dragon!

Jacob Patmore (9)
The Harrodian School, Barnes

Bus Kids

I am strolling along on my way to school.
The sun is bright but there is a chill in the air.
I have plenty of time and not a care in the world,
When suddenly I hear a rolling rumble.

In the distance a scarlet giant is growing.
It is coming at me with many heads.
It grows larger and louder
And comes between me and the gate.

I have to run for it!
The giant opens its mouth and spills out its children.
They swarm and scatter and swallow me up.
I get pushed and pulled and graze my elbow and knee.
They spit me out at the door,
All battered and bruised.

That's what it is like when the Bus Kids come.

Imagen Powell (8)
The Harrodian School, Barnes

Witches At Hallowe'en

W arts on ugly, wrinkly faces.
 I nside the cauldron there is bubbling frogs' legs.
 T rembling children trick or treat through the night.
 C ats as black as a starless night.
 H ats as pointy as a knife.
 E vil cackling witches soar through the night.
 S ticky, white, glowing cobwebs crawling with black spiders.

Charlotte Birtles (9)
The Harrodian School, Barnes

You

You're as useless . . .
As a tongue without a lick.
As a foot without a kick.
As a bowl without a fish.
As a fairy without a wish.

As useless . . .
As a drip without a drop.
As a flip without a flop.
As a dog without a bark.
As a night that is not dark.

As useless . . .
As a singer without a song.
As a gong without a bong.
As a lock without a key.
In fact you're almost as useless as me.

Charlie Nason (10)
The Harrodian School, Barnes

Big Burt

Big Burt sat on a cushion,
'I'm much too fat,' moaned he,
'Who else could be so miserable?'
The cushion answered, 'Me!'
Burt said, 'I'm really rather sorry,
I can't help being big.'
'Why don't you go to Weight Watchers
Or go on a diet of fig?'
So Big Burt went on his diet
And became extremely thin.
The cushion though was very sad,
'What's become of him?'

Zoë Spurgeon (9)
The Harrodian School, Barnes

Useless

You're as useless . . .
As a witch without her broom,
As me without my room,
As a school without chairs,
As a house without stairs.

As useless . . .
As paper without the pen,
As a chicken without the hen,
As Chessington without the rides,
As the groom without the bride.

As useless . . .
As a beach without the sea,
As a beehive without the bee,
As a leg without the knee,
In fact you're as useless as me.

Sasha Vergopoulos (10)
The Harrodian School, Barnes

Olivia

O is for optimistic, sunny and bright
L is for lively, I just can't sit tight
I is for intelligent, just bearing fruit
V is for van Meeteren, my Dutch roots
I is for independent, doing my own thing
A is for adventures and happy endings.

Olivia van Meeteren (9)
The Harrodian School, Barnes

Autumn

Autumn's winds are rough and breezy
They make my brother a little queasy
The leaves begin to fall off the trees
As I jump into the sea
Tough and cold is the water
I think I found some money, a quarter
I see some people wearing their coats
While I am on a summer float
I see flowers die and cripple
I hear someone play the fiddle
To chase away the wasps nest
Autumn's season is the best.

Aimee Van der Merwe (10)
The Harrodian School, Barnes

Useless

You're as useless . . .

As a sun with no light
As a man that isn't bright
As a witch with no broom
As a cat which isn't groomed

As a gift given free
As useless as mini me
As a boy that doesn't say please
As a very melted piece of cheese.

Luke Finckenstein (10)
The Harrodian School, Barnes

Useless

You're as useless . . .
As Hallowe'en without a scare
As a werewolf without its hair
As a witch without a broom
As a mummy without a tomb.

As useless . . .
As a skeleton without its bones
As a zombie without its moans
As a haunted house without its bats
As a scary clown without its hats.

As useless . . .
As a sunken ship out at sea
As a painful dislocated knee
As a crooked front door without a key
In fact you're just as useless as me.

Edward Cadbury (10)
The Harrodian School, Barnes

Friendship

Friendship is as strong as super glue
And as deep as the oceans
It carries us over hard points in life
And gives us comfort when we are in fight
Friendship is a prized possession
Although it is free
Friendship is the best
For you and me.

Connie O'Neill (10)
The Harrodian School, Barnes

Useless

You're as useless as . . .
A beach without warm sand
All the crushed elastic bands
As a farmer without a farm
As a lamb without a barn.

You're as useless . . .
As a sky without the clouds
As a boat without the sea
As a man without his cap
As a tree without the sap.

You're as useless . . .
As a money note without the shine
As a sweet without the wrapper
A cup without its tea
You're as useless as me!

Isabella Gasparro (10)
The Harrodian School, Barnes

Bush Fires

Fires leap along the bushes
Flames crackle and cackle
Devouring the trees
Daring to go further

Swallowing leaves
Spitting out sparks
Fireballs jumping away casually
Skipping around the bushes

Sophia Brown (10)
The Harrodian School, Barnes

You're As Useless As A . . .

You're as useless . . .
As a dog without a bone
As a human with a clone
As a sweet shop that is closed
As a guard who's had a doze.

As useless . . .
As a snail that has shrunk
As a bed without a bunk
As a tree without a trunk
As a chav who isn't a punk.

As useless . . .
As a lion without a roar
As a dog without a paw
As a plane without its wings
As a country with no kings.

Toby Watson (10)
The Harrodian School, Barnes

Useless

You're as useless . . .
As a stream without its flow
As a sewer not down low
As London without the Thames
As a camera without a lens.

As useless . . .
As seaweed not in sea
As a leaf without a tree
As a frozen cup of tea
In fact you're almost as useless as me.

Enora Seite (10)
The Harrodian School, Barnes

Useless

You're as useless . . .
As a chair without its legs
As a clothes line without its pegs
As a fish without his gills
As a packet without the pills.

You're as useless . . .
As a computer without the mouse
As a person without her house
As a sea that's not blue
As a flush without the loo.

You're as useless . . .
As a phone without its ring
As a bell without a ding
As an eye that can't see
You're almost as useless as me!

Sophie Lynn (10)
The Harrodian School, Barnes

Useless

You're as useless . . .
As a bone with no socket
As trousers with no pocket
As a balloon with no air
As a bear with no hair.

As useless . . .
As a nest without birds
As a book with no words
As a cold cup of tea
As a clone of me.

Charlie Whitfield (10)
The Harrodian School, Barnes

Regal Tricks

The king and queen were very royal,
A very regal pair,
They made their subjects' spirits boil
Because they loved to scare.
Their prized possession was their daughter
Who they scared with a very loud sound,
But as she often stood by water she very nearly drowned!

'On them we need to play a trick,'
The royal daughter said.
'Above their door I'll place a brick
Which will fall upon their head.'

The door was opened, the brick fell down
Just missing the regal head.
'No more tricks for me,' he said.
'I was very nearly dead!'

Anthea Themistocleous (9)
The Harrodian School, Barnes

The Tornado

Again and again,
It coughs up a swirling mass of destruction,
Howling its war cries to the ears of the world.
It sprints across the land, leaving a trail of putrid and
                                        homeless misery.

Again and again,
With a flick of a finger the land crumbles beneath its feet.
People lose everything they care for beneath its mighty roar.
Debris takes flight in the atmosphere, only to crash back down
                                        to Earth,

As gravity takes its toll.

Lauren Milner (10)
The Harrodian School, Barnes

The Amazing Feeling

I feel a sparkle growing inside of me.
I feel like a firework, popping and crackling with joy.
I feel like the ocean, calmly swaying with peace.
I feel a type of weather, the sun when I am happy
And rain when I am sad.
I feel like a flower, blossoming with scent.
I feel like a fire burning and making me warm.
I feel like silk, smooth and soft letting me calm someone down
with a gentle hug.
I feel like a model, showing my sense of style.
As I drift off to sleep,
I imagine what I feel.

Claudia Telling (9)
The Harrodian School, Barnes

A Tsunami

Again and again . . .
The water gargles and slurps.
Then you see a humongous wave, running on the water,
Slurping the water in its way.
All the humans on the beach run crazy all around,
The tsunami swallows the houses. It's gone momentarily . . .

Again and again . . .
You hear the water gargle longer, longer away.
The water gets sneezed back again.
Now the humans prepare themselves to build a new country . . .

Ebba Berggren (11)
The Harrodian School, Barnes

Useless

You're as useless . . .
As a shoe without a sock
As a key without a lock
As a board without a pen
As a bear without a den.

As useless . . .
As a ship without a sail
As a shout without a wail
As a mouth without some spit
As a fire which is not lit.

As useless . . .
As a glass without a drink
As a TV without a link
As a door without a knob
As a corn without a cob.

As useless . . .
As a board without a wave
As a bear without a cave
As a gift that isn't free
In fact you're almost as useless as me.

Maud Gaynor (10)
The Harrodian School, Barnes

The Snake

The super-smooth snake sneaks
Slyly, stupidly
With its aim
To slay its prey
It succeeds and
Leaves sizzling sand
In its wake
In the shape of a snake.

Lucy Grinnan (10)
The Harrodian School, Barnes

Useless

You're as useless . . .
As a star without its fame,
As a horse without its mane,
As a sledge without its snow,
As a flower that can't grow!

You're as useless . . .
As a door without its knob,
As a burglar that doesn't rob,
As a sword without its sharpness,
As a room without darkness!

You're as useless . . .
As a sweet without its taste,
As a brush without its paste,
As honey without a bee,
You're as useless as me!

Alexia Van Breugel (10)
The Harrodian School, Barnes

Useless

You're as useless as . . .
A TV with no channels
As a bath with no flannels
As some ice without liquid
As the sea without its squid

As a cat without a tail
As a shell without a snail
As a chip with no ketchup
As some stairs you can't go up.

Wilfred Dutton (10)
The Harrodian School, Barnes

Sweets

I munch and I crunch until my molars go yellow.
I munch and I crunch until my legs are marshmallows.
I munch and I crunch all I've seen.
I munch and I crunch until my face is green.
I munch and I crunch . . . *blaaagh!*

Fiona Donald (9)
The Harrodian School, Barnes

Whirlpool

As the whirlpool spins round and round it sucks in everything
Sucking ships to the murky depths
It has no mercy as it spins round
When the whirlpool has calmed the things you lost
You will never get back
From the merciless depths of the whirlpool.

Edmund Slimmon (11)
The Harrodian School, Barnes

Tornado

The wind dances, spinning like a black hole
Across the summer's parched fields
Swallowing up cars and coughing them out
Into the cowering sky
Devouring everything.

Jake Meakin & Sonya Djemal (10)
The Harrodian School, Barnes

Useless

You're as useless as a football without its players,
You're as useless as the world without life,
You're as useless as food without an eater,
You're as useless as a car without its wheels,
You're as useless as a chimney without a fire,
You're as useless as a DVD player without a DVD,
You're as useless as a nit without hair.

Harry Picken (10)
The Harrodian School, Barnes

Lazy Days

Lazy's colour is like light blue with violet,
Lazy tastes like hot lasagne,
Lazy smells like warm chicken casserole,
Lazy looks like a forty-inch television,
Lazy sound like an old man snoring,
Lazy feels like a woolly rug.

Louis Ravens (9)
The Harrodian School, Barnes

Scary Thoughts

Scary is black like a bat flying at night.
Scary tastes like chocolate in scrambled eggs.
Scary smells like World War II trenches.
Scary looks like a gloomy ghost.
Scary sounds like creaky stairs.
Scary feels like a vampire biting you.

Thomas Hill (9)
The Harrodian School, Barnes

Useless

You're as useless as . . . .
An iPod with no songs
A ding without a dong
A cat without a mouse
A door without a house

You're as useless as . . .
Honey without a bee
A teapot with no tea
The alphabet without the letter D
In fact you're almost as useless as me.

Evie Henderson (10)
The Harrodian School, Barnes

Depressed Poem

Depression is grey like a foggy winter's day,
It tastes like off milk,
It smells like old perfume,
It feels like being all alone,
It sounds quiet.

Isla Rose Hodsoll (9)
The Harrodian School, Barnes

Dream Box

I have a dream box for putting dreams in.
I put the nightmares in the bin,
To save the good ones for rainy days,
So I can dream them again and again.
I like my dream box very much,
The dreams tickle my fingers whenever I touch.
I open it up when it gets dark,
Ready for my dream in the park.
If you had a dream box too,
I'm sure you'd be as happy as me too!

Phoebe Abbott (11)
The Harrodian School, Barnes

At My Door

There was a cat stood at my door.
There was a cat and nothing more.
Its fur was shining in the stars.
Among the stars there was Mars.

Mars was red like burning fire gazing at my door.
Mars was crying shining tears that fell right through the universe.
The universe was at my door,
The universe . . . *and nothing more!*

Lily Siddiqi (10)
The Harrodian School, Barnes

Useless

You're as useless as . . .
A pig without a nose
A model without a pose
A garden without a hose

A room without a socket
Trousers without a pocket
A necklace without a locket.

Saskia Fitzpatrick (10)
The Harrodian School, Barnes

Tsunami Attack

The sea gets slurped up by a giant spiralling straw
Spat out to devour its prey
Engulfing the plants and houses
Sucking them up like a vacuum.

Saskia Moyle (10)
The Harrodian School, Barnes

Food For All Seasons

I like the changing seasons,
Spring, summer, autumn, even winter.
Each time of year a different food to eat,
In spring, when the buds are newly spread
And birds look from their nests
I like pasta, grilled fish and chocolate mousse.

In summer, when the sun shines bright
And days are long
I like cold drinks, barbecues and sweet ice cream.

In autumn, when golden leaves softly fall
And farmers bring in the harvest
I like sausage and bacon, apples and plums.

In winter, when furry creatures go to sleep
And curl beneath bare trees
I like hot chocolate and Christmas turkey, although I'm not so keen
on sprouts!

I like summer best of all
When I can swim and play all day
And eat and drink my favourite things.

Daniel Marchand (9)
The Harrodian School, Barnes

The Holy Grail Of Bananas

Humour is like ice creams falling from the sky
It is a rainbow of colour on a candy cane
It tastes of freshly baked croissants
And blackberry and apple pies
It smells of a world of melting chocolate
It sounds like children sucking lollipops
It makes me think of happy things like delicious roast lunches.

Tiernan O'Brien (9)
The Harrodian School, Barnes

When I Grow Up

When I grow up
I hope to be two feet taller
When I grow up
I hope to become a great tennis player

When I grow up
I will own a big Roller
When I grow up
I can also become a bowler

When I grow up
I will grow a big moustache
When I grow up
I hope to earn a lot of cash

When I grow up
I will have a big bash
When I grow up
My days will always start with a big splash!

Leo Cranmer (10)
The Harrodian School, Barnes

My Dog Minni

My dog Minni, I don't what she is,
Is she a dog or is she a ball of fizz?
When I come home from school she runs to me like a horse
And kisses my face with amazing force.

My dog Minni makes me smile when I'm sad,
She nibbles my nose and I don't feel bad.
She's a mixture of features,
Unique amongst creatures.

My dog Minni, she is so fine
And best of all she's all mine!

Jack Godik (10)
The Harrodian School, Barnes

Useless

You're as useless . . .
As a world without people
As a cat that isn't nimble, nimble
As a clock without a face
As a shoe without a lace.

You're as useless . . .
As a house without a floor
As a room without a door
As a guitar without a string
As a chav without some bling.

You're as useless . . .
As an athlete without legs
As a clothes line without pegs
As some fish without the sea
In fact you're almost as useless as me.

Perry Saxon (10)
The Harrodian School, Barnes

A Joy Poem

One sunny day I felt all blue around,
I tasted fresh air gushing in on me.
It smelt home-made and fresh.
It looked like kids running out of school.
It sounded like waves crashing in the breeze.
It felt calm.

Eleanor Clare Morgan (9)
The Harrodian School, Barnes

My Brother

My brother Albie is a nightmare,
He has a snotty nose and sticky up hair.

He kicks my dog and breaks my toys
And all day long makes so much noise.

He makes me want to climb the wall,
When he always plays and acts the fool.

When he's hurt he wants his dummy
And cries all the time for our mummy.

But even though he annoys me so,
I would miss him if he were ever to go.

Delilah Saxena (9)
The Harrodian School, Barnes

Hallowe'en

Pumpkins, pumpkins in a row,
A guideline for the witches as they go,
Children knock on doors for treats,
They never know who they might meet.

Full moon, howling wolves,
Bubbling cauldrons and witches brew,
Hallowe'en's coming beware . . .

Hannah Symonds (9)
The Harrodian School, Barnes

Peace

Peace is a shiny blue.
Peace smells of sweet strawberries.
Peace is an everlasting cycle of life.
Peace sounds like the wind.
Peace tastes like chocolate ice cream.

Chris McNaught (9)
The Harrodian School, Barnes

My Furry Friend

I have a cat who is my furry friend,
She is my furry alarm clock
Who wakes me up when the night ends.
She is as soft as a gigantic pillow.
She is as beautiful as a big willow.
She is as lively as a buzzing bee.
She really has got big green eyes that help her see.
I love my furry friend and there is a lot of love that she sends.

Millie Davis (9)
The Harrodian School, Barnes

The Colosseum

Do you think the Colosseum is only a museum?
Did you know that in days long gone
Gladiators fought creatures wild and strong?
The life of the brave was decided on by the Emperor's thumb -
Right or wrong!
If the thumb goes down your life is gone!
But if it points up you will be free for long.

Johannes Henkel (9)
The Harrodian School, Barnes

Spooky

The door was black and it had cracks in it,
The air tasted damp and wet,
The smell was gruesome like ghosts breathing down your neck,
The room was dark and empty,
It sounded like somebody was rocking up and down,
Up and down on a rocking chair.

Milo Draco (10)
The Harrodian School, Barnes

True Love

Princess Emma gazed out her window and wiped away a tear,
When a knight in shining armour shouted, 'Do not fear.'
He called out, 'I have come to save you, come with me if you dare,
Now let me take you away from this wizard's dreadful lair.'
The princess did not fight
And like a magnet ran to meet her knight,
The horse that he rode on was a golden sunny light,
So they galloped off together until day turned to night.
They sped towards his castle like a cheetah hunting prey,
But they did not know where their future lay.
Then one night his life did dart,
As a silver knife went through his heart.
No one knew who did the deed,
Maybe the wizard out of greed.
The princess who was shattered drew a knife into her chest,
And plunged it down her very best,
They met at once in Heaven on high,
Where everyone goes when they die,
And there they stand to this very day,
Holding hands hip hip hooray!

Philippa Nowikow (9)
The Harrodian School, Barnes

Do Colours Have Meanings?

Red is the sign of danger.
I see red, I feel anger.
Blue is cold icy water running into a lake and bright skies shining.
I see blue, I feel peaceful.
Green is the colour of life jumping into action and growing grass.
I see green, I feel lively.
Black is dark and a scary feeling running through my body.
I see black, I feel frightened.
Yellow is the colour of creation and new life.
I see yellow, I feel happy.

Grace Walker (9)
The Harrodian School, Barnes

Finishing Line

A sprinter is a cheetah running across the finishing line,
A swimmer is like a fast fish in the blue water,
A pole-vaulter is a hare's legs leaping to catch its prey,
A wrestler is like a huge elephant squashing anyone in its way,
A gymnast is a snake slithering in the flat desert,
A rower is like a beautiful swan gliding across the shimmering water.

Claudia Talbot (9)
The Harrodian School, Barnes

The Love Poem

Love is red like a beating heart.
It tastes as sweet as strawberry and fizzy champagne.
It smells like a dark red rose.
It looks as lovely as a red heart.
It sounds as if it will last forever.
It feels as comfy as lying in a heart-shaped bed.

Trinny Phillips (10)
The Harrodian School, Barnes

Busy

I think I am a muffin man,
I don't have a bell,
I haven't got the muffin things that muffin people sell.

I think I am a postman,
No a tram,
I am feeling rather funny and I don't know what I am!

Emma Wilson (9)
The Harrodian School, Barnes

Scary

It is red like fire,
It tastes like mouldy old fish,
It smells like horrible blue cheese,
It looks like an arm crawling along the floor,
It sounds like a wolf howling at midnight,
It feels like someone chopping off my head.

Noah Russell (10)
The Harrodian School, Barnes

The Wild

W ildebeests run away,
I ce foxes run for their prey,
L ions are the kings of the jungle,
D angerous vultures flap their wings.

Maggie Pound (9)
The Harrodian School, Barnes

The Olympic Games

A sprinter is a car at top speed.
A pole-vaulter is a kangaroo, legs leaping.
A swimmer is a fish swimming through the ocean.
A weightlifter is a very annoyed ape.
A gymnast is a flexible ruler.

Jessy McCabe (9)
The Harrodian School, Barnes

December

December
   December is a cold month
   December is a fun month
   December is a good month

December
   December is Christmas month
   December is a popular month
   December is a family month

December
   December is the best month
   December is a kind month
   December is a crystal month

December
   December is our month
   December is my month
   December is a musical month

December
   December is a special month
   December is a merry and bright month

December
   December is Jesus' birth month
   December is my birthday month
   December is a merry month.

Camille Waugh (10)
Trinity St Mary's CE Primary School, Balham

Life

Life is a misery that none can solve,
You always get up whenever you're told.
Chanté get up! Chanté do your homework!
Chanté go in the bath! Chanté go to bed!
Chanté get ready! Chanté go to school!

And when I get to school,
My teacher says, 'Chanté come in!
Chanté do your work! Chanté have you finished?
Chanté where's your homework! Chanté detention!
Chanté come to class! Chanté go to lunch!'

And when I do my best my teacher says, 'Well done
Chanté you are marvellous!
Chanté you are great! Chanté you're a team player!
Chanté you're a good mate!'

Chanté Leander (10)
Trinity St Mary's CE Primary School, Balham

Rats

Some rats are fast,
Some rats are slow,
White, black, brown off they go,
When you see them you will know.

Some rats are fat,
Some rats are slim,
When you see them they will jump up and down,
At great speed you will run.

Whitney Houston (10)
Trinity St Mary's CE Primary School, Balham

Ghana 2K7

Ghana, Ghana in the air
Ghana, Ghana everywhere
When I'm walking down the street
I love the smell of your fresh cooked meat

Pretty girls and arrogant men
Girls normally plucking hens
Ghana here, Ghana there
Love girls' great braided hair.

Traditional flag, gold and green
If you're naughty people get mean
Then there is red with a black star
You don't know how important you are

You can be bad but mostly good
I am bad, I grew up in this hood
Ghana, Ghana how are you?
Ghana I miss you!

Kwesi Mensah (10)
Trinity St Mary's CE Primary School, Balham

Birds

Birds are rude
Birds are crude
Birds can fly
Birds can lie
Birds can sing
Birds can spring
Birds are red
Birds get fed
But best of all . . .
Birds are cool.

Aaron McCubbin (10)
Trinity St Mary's CE Primary School, Balham

Bumblebees

Bumblebees flying here and there
They've got yellow and black stripes
And really thick hair

They've got really cool wings and sticky legs
They've got really small heads
And they look like wooden pegs

Bumblebees buzz in your ear
You try to swat them
But they never fear

They can sting you
Like a really sharp knife
If they get your brain or your heart
You will lose your life

Bumblebees are really great
They are fast and smart
They can be your mate.

Ayo Ogunyoye (11)
Trinity St Mary's CE Primary School, Balham

Colours

Roses are red, violets are blue,
All the colours of the rainbow are colourful!
Colours are pink, orange, black,
Purple, brown, some are bright
And some are dark,
But we all like pretty colours!
Colours are bright,
Colours are dark and dull
But we all like pretty colours!
Colours are fun.
Colours, colours so beautiful indeed!
Colours, colours amazing and so beautiful!

Serena Edwards (10)
Trinity St Mary's CE Primary School, Balham

George The Ape

George the ape who wears a black and white cape,
Travels through his homeland which is brown and green,
But when he takes a shower there is lots of steam,
He goes out hunting for his family to stay alive
And when he goes fishing he loves to take a dive.

George the ape who wears a black and white cape,
He travels through the city, never feels pity.
When he is in a good mood he always catches food,
When he's not he only catches turtle trot.

George the ape who wears a black and white cape,
When he comes home he loves to roam,
When he is in his jungle place there is nothing but jungle safe,
No bears, no tigers, no dangerous fish,
If there were they would be down in a ditch.

George the ape who wears a black and white cape.

Timi Ogunyoye (10)
Trinity St Mary's CE Primary School, Balham

Rainbow Colours

R ainbows make people smile and laugh,
A s they float high in the sky.
I t's in the autumn that you see them the most.
N umerous colours fill the air,
B eautiful colours everywhere.
O range is the second one and it's also the brightest one.
W ell now you know what I think about rainbows.

C oloured patterns are in the air,
O range, yellow and blue everywhere.
L ittle things make me smile,
O nce in a while.
U se an umbrella, use a fan,
R ainbows are joyful things but
S uddenly they float away and now there's not much laughter
and play.

Karolina Bakun (10)
Trinity St Mary's CE Primary School, Balham

Mythological Creatures

Mythological creatures, are they real or fake?
No one's ever seen them or so people say.
I believe they are real somewhere in a cave.
Fairies, pixies and giants, I believe in them all, whether they are
                                                        big or small.
Mermaids live in the sea and I think a griffin would live in a tree.
I would love to be a fairy,
All small and twinkly.

Witches make me laugh with their horrible green skin.
I love the way a unicorn gallops in the moonlight,
I wish I knew if they were real or not.
They seem so nice to be gobbled up.
I think a pixie would be tastiest, and a giant would taste of bitterness.
A troll would be sour, and a mermaid would be sweet.
Which one would you eat?

Lily Du (10)
Trinity St Mary's CE Primary School, Balham

Colours

Colours, colours everywhere,
Colours, colours in your hair.
Colours, colours black and blue,
Colours, colours are on you.

Colours, colours purple and white,
Colours, colours dull and bright.
Colours, colours brown and pink,
Colours, colours make you think.

Colours, colours green and red,
Colours, colours make you want to go to bed.
Colours, colours silver and gold,
Colours, colours make you cold.

Darnel Williams (10)
Trinity St Mary's CE Primary School, Balham

A Trip To Jupiter

I boarded the Eurostar at Waterloo,
I was so excited
I didn't know what to do.

The train started to go
My thoughts began to flow
To Paris on the Eurostar
But no we went to Jupiter.

We went past Mars,
We met an alien called Zars
He got a ticket and jumped on-board
But was chucked off for pulling the emergency cord.

Jupiter was in our sights,
We saw a fiery storm,
The train turned back it was so bright,
Orange and red round planet.

Back to Waterloo we went,
Where shall we go tomorrow?

Lewis Howard (10)
Trinity St Mary's CE Primary School, Balham

Racism

You don't belong here people
If you're not going to treat us equal

It's people like we can't trust
Treating us illegal isn't a must

It happens if you're black, it happens if you're white
But in any case racism it is never right

We do belong here
We have a family tree
England is our home country

It's true, not a lie
Because people still die

Shienika Haughton (11)
Trinity St Mary's CE Primary School, Balham

Monkeys

Monkeys are bad,
Monkeys are rude,
See them eating bananas
And throwing their food.

Chittering, chattering,
Jumping around
Those cheeky monkeys
Making monkey sounds.

From branch to branch
They swing and play,
Having lots of fun
Every day.

If I was an animal,
Guess what I'd be?
I would be
A monkey
You see.

Shaquilla Gordon (10)
Trinity St Mary's CE Primary School, Balham

Darkness

Darkness is black like burning charcoal.
Darkness tastes like sour raspberries.
Darkness feels like smooth pieces of cold metal.
Darkness sounds like the rustle of leaves.
Darkness smells like melting plastic.
Darkness looks like a deep, dark, empty hole.
Darkness reminds me of a silent room.

Danielle Wiles (10)
Trinity St Mary's CE Primary School, Balham

Christmas

Christmas, Christmas you're so fun,
Christmas, Christmas you're colder than a cold bun.
Christmas, Christmas with angels and stars,
Christmas, Christmas you're better than Mars bars.

Christmas, Christmas with Christmas trees,
Christmas, Christmas you hardly see any bees.
Christmas, Christmas with tasty food,
Christmas, Christmas you put me in the right mood.

Christmas, Christmas with all the presents,
Christmas, Christmas it's all really pleasant.
Christmas, Christmas I love you,
Christmas, Christmas no one says *boo* to you.

Christmas, Christmas I'm so glad,
Christmas, Christmas you're not bad.
Christmas, Christmas I have a wonderful time,
Christmas, Christmas I would like to drink some wine.

Ayomiposi Onajide (10)
Trinity St Mary's CE Primary School, Balham

Summer

S un you are so bright and hot, come to my house, you will love
it a lot.
U se an umbrella to get shade from the summer.
M other let me jump into a pool and bring towels with you.
M outh you are so precious, fresh water is so delicious.
E xtremely hot and boiling, a fan will be good to keep me cooler.
R ed sun you're so bright I wish you came at night.

Joshua Liverpool (11)
Trinity St Mary's CE Primary School, Balham

Animals, Animals Everywhere

There are many animals,
Here, there and everywhere,
They're on your sofa, under your bed, even on your bottom stair.
They're absolutely everywhere.

My favourite is the cat,
Watch as he prances on his mat.
I also like dogs
And sometimes even hedgehogs.
See I told you animals are everywhere,
Absolutely everywhere.

Sophie Sinclair-West (10)
Trinity St Mary's CE Primary School, Balham

Ice

I like cold stuff, especially ice cream dripping from my mouth.
C ream so nice and soft it makes me feel like eating candyfloss.
E at some cold ice and your teeth will chatter and you won't eat
ice ever again.

Grace Ottinah (10)
Trinity St Mary's CE Primary School, Balham

Season - Spring and Summer

S pring is the time when flowers blossom and germinate
E veryone is out admiring their gardens very late
A nimals small like bees land elegantly on flowers
S ummer comes straight after spring ends
O utside the sun shines high in the sky
N ow we all leave to go to the beach to fly our kites.

Emmanuella Abraham (10)
Trinity St Mary's CE Primary School, Balham

My Favourite Dream

Grass is green
Fire is red
I don't go to school
When I dream in my bed.

I am a boy of ten
I started school at three
My teachers were cool
Just like me.

Kings and queens
Would add you to their list
Cut your head off
And rule with an iron fist.

Marlon Mitchell (10)
Trinity St Mary's CE Primary School, Balham

Fear

Fear sounds like someone shouting.
Fear tastes like blood.
Fear smells like fire and smoke.
Fear looks like RIP.
Fear feels like horror.
Fear reminds me of spring.

Eugenio Marletta (7)
Trinity St Mary's CE Primary School, Balham

Love

Love sounds like a heavenly angel singing.
Love tastes like juicy strawberries.
Love smells like heavenly rose perfume.
Love looks like a red heart growing.
Love looks like jumping over the moon.
Love reminds me of Cupid.

Jackson Rouse (7)
Trinity St Mary's CE Primary School, Balham

Love

Love sounds like the golden wedding bells.
Love tastes like a chocolate bunny and roses.
Love smells like a heavenly rose perfume.
Love looks like a wedding ring.
Love feels like a gentle kiss.
Love reminds me of sweet kisses.

Hazzan Olalemi (7)
Trinity St Mary's CE Primary School, Balham

Love

Love sounds like your mummy saying, 'I love you.'
Love tastes like a rainbow lollipop.
Love smells like a bunch of red and pink roses.
Love looks like children kissing their moms.
Love feels like an exciting, loving world.
Love reminds me of my best friends.

Courteney Welch (7)
Trinity St Mary's CE Primary School, Balham

Happiness

Happiness sounds like people playing.
Happiness tastes like a lovely pink cake.
Happiness smells like the delicious strawberries.
Happiness looks like people smiling.
Happiness feels like somebody is hugging you.
Happiness reminds me of my old friends.

Stephanie Burrows (8)
Trinity St Mary's CE Primary School, Balham

Fun

Fun is multicoloured like Smarties scattered along the ground.
Fun sounds like someone is getting tickled to laughter.
Fun smells like chocolate melted in your hands.
Fun looks like jumping in a jacuzzi.
Fun feels like staying up late.
Fun reminds me of going to a birthday party.
Fun, fun, fun.
Fun tastes like eating fudge all day long.

Samiat Oke (9)
Trinity St Mary's CE Primary School, Balham

Silence

Silence is pink like fluffy cotton candy.
Silence smells like fresh air on a summer's day.
Silence feels like there's nobody there but an invisible ball.
Silence looks like there's nothing there but a wall.
Silence reminds me of light up above.
Silence sounds like a pin dropping to the ground.

Destene Leslie-Myrie (9)
Trinity St Mary's CE Primary School, Balham

Fun

Fun is multicoloured like Smarties scattered along the floor.
Fun sounds like children screaming and hurting themselves.
Fun tastes like different artificial-coloured fish fingers.
Fun smells like fresh flowers in the sky.
Fun looks like balloons in people's hands.
Fun feels like soft fur.
Fun reminds me about the good times. Yeah.

Darnell Nelson (9)
Trinity St Mary's CE Primary School, Balham

Silence

Silence is dead black like coal.
Silence reminds me of a boy sitting on a chair.
Silence tastes like wonderful air.
Silence smells like a million angels.
Silence feels like snow falling on me.
Silence looks like a small child making a wish.
Silence sounds like a boy sleeping on Christmas Eve.

Linno Lukebanu (9)
Trinity St Mary's CE Primary School, Balham

Silence

Silence is white like a clear breezy meadow.
Silence sounds like you're just in a plain room.
Silence tastes like medicine with no taste.
Silence smells like nothing.
Silence looks like an invisible poem.
Silence feels like you are standing in the middle of nowhere.
Silence reminds me of Remembrance Day.

Jeshaiah Olowu (9)
Trinity St Mary's CE Primary School, Balham

Silence

Silence is white like a bunch of clouds.
Silence smells like fresh air.
Silence tastes like water coming out the air.
Silence feels like you're alone in a dark corner.
Silence looks like wind passing right past you.
Silence reminds me of when I was alone.

Kaysharna McIntosh (9)
Trinity St Mary's CE Primary School, Balham

Darkness

Darkness is pitch-black like you're under a cover of nothing,
Darkness sounds of peace and loneliness,
Darkness tastes like a whirlwind of smoke,
Darkness smells like a cold small box of steam,
Darkness feels like you are floating through thin fluffy clouds,
Darkness reminds me of an empty cave,
Darkness looks like the night sky, still and silent.

Brianna Rouse (9)
Trinity St Mary's CE Primary School, Balham

Laughter

Laughter is blue like a big wavy river.
Laughter sounds like a fat horse laughing.
Laughter tastes like crunchy biscuits.
Laughter smells like minty toothpaste.
Laughter looks like a funny jumping clown.
Laughter feels like a soft dog.
Laughter reminds me of happy times.

Kamile Adomaitis (9)
Trinity St Mary's CE Primary School, Balham

Hunger

Hunger is orange like thin little carrots.
Hunger sounds like tiny hungry mice.
Hunger tastes like an empty white plate.
Hunger smells like a dry hot dessert.
Hunger feels like a shrivelled empty stomach.
Hunger reminds me of a starving child.

Elayne Freeman (9)
Trinity St Mary's CE Primary School, Balham

Darkness

Darkness is black like a deep fierce forest.
Darkness sounds like the owls in a tree.
Darkness tastes like thin air.
Darkness smells like the plain sky.
Darkness looks like blackness.
Darkness feels like someone touching me.
Darkness reminds me of my bed.

Ammoy Campbell (9)
Trinity St Mary's CE Primary School, Balham

Darkness

Darkness is dark like a black mysterious alleyway.
Darkness sounds silent *tick-tock, tick-tock.*
Darkness tastes bitter like a sour sweet.
Darkness smells like fresh blood.
Darkness looks pitch-black.
Darkness feels like walking into Hell.
Darkness reminds me of being in my grave.

Ovigwe Eyarhono (10)
Trinity St Mary's CE Primary School, Balham

Darkness

Darkness is black like when you're under a duvet.
Darkness sounds like a kangaroo.
Darkness tastes like a leaf that's ripe.
Darkness smells like God sleeping.
Darkness looks like a huge empty cardboard box.
Darkness feels like a dream man.
Darkness reminds me of spaceships and stars.

Taran Feaver (9)
Trinity St Mary's CE Primary School, Balham

Young Writers Information

We hope you have enjoyed reading this book - and that you will continue to enjoy it in the coming years.

If you like reading and writing poetry drop us a line, or give us a call, and we'll send you a free information pack.

Alternatively if you would like to order further copies of this book or any of our other titles, then please give us a call or log onto our website at www.youngwriters.co.uk

Young Writers Information
Remus House
Coltsfoot Drive
Peterborough
PE2 9JX

(01733) 890066